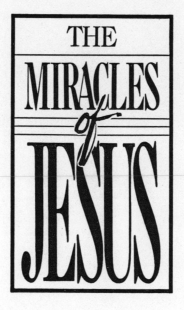

THE
MIRACLES
of
JESUS

THE MIRACLES of JESUS

While this book is intended for the reader's personal enjoyment and profit, it is also intended for group study. A leader's guide with Reproducible Response Sheets is available from your local bookstore or from the publisher.

LESLIE B. FLYNN

Unless otherwise noted, Scripture quotations are from the *King James Version.* Other quotations are from the *Revised Standard Version of the Bible* (RSV), © 1946, 1952, 1971, 1973; *The Living Bible* (TLB), © 1971, Tyndale House Publishers, Wheaton, IL 60189; and the *Holy Bible, New International Version* (NIV), © 1973, 1978, 1984, International Bible Society. Used by permission of Zondervan Bible Publishers.

Flynn, Leslie B.
  The miracles of Jesus/Leslie B. Flynn.
    p. cm.
  ISBN 0-89693-749-6
  1. Jesus Christ—Miracles. I. Title.
BT366.F49 1990
232.9'55—dc20

2 3 4 5 6 7 8 9 10 Printing/Year 94 93 92 91 90

CONTENTS

FOREWORD

I n His healing ministry the Lord Jesus Christ had a 100-percent success rate. He healed all who came seeking health. With a mere touch or a firm command, without medical treatment, or delay of convalescence, the paralyzed walked, the blind received sight, the lepers were cleansed, and the demon-possessed were cured. He was the Super Healer in a class all by Himself.

Not only did Jesus heal, but He also performed other miracles, showing His power over nature and over death. Roughly 30 percent of Mark's Gospel alone deals directly or indirectly with miracles. The multitudes marveled at Jesus' authority.

Though He healed all who sought wellness, He did not heal every ailing individual in Judea and Galilee. And those He did heal later fell ill and died. Their miraculous renewal of health was not permanent in this world. Why did He heal them when He knew they would decline in health and die later—and when He knew that their eternal life was far more important than their physical well-being? This book offers an answer to that question.

Today we use the word *miracle* loosely and include under its umbrella anything unusual or supernatural. However, the New Testament meaning of *miracle* requires a much more restricted usage. This book deals with the narrower definition.

Rather than discussing each of the 35 recorded miracles of Jesus separately, we will deal with them in three major categories: nature, healings, and resurrections.

For example, the nine nature miracles break down into five groupings: fish (three miracles), storms (two), feedings of multitudes (two), the withering of a fig tree (one), and water into wine (one). We devote a chapter to each of the five groupings.

7

FOREWORD

The 23 healings fall into four major classes and a few minor ones. The most repeated areas of healing are demon-possession, blindness, impairment of limbs like paralysis or lameness, and leprosy. We devote a chapter to each of these types, another arbitrarily to the healing of the woman with an issue of blood, and still another to the three resurrections. Though we omit the cures of dropsy, fever, deafness, and muteness, plus the healing of the high priest's servant's ear sliced off by Peter, we nevertheless mention in some way a majority of the occasions in which the Healer worked a wonder.

What lessons do the miracles of Jesus have for us today? The introductory chapter presents five areas of significance. However, this book emphasizes their symbolic purpose of portraying redemptive truths. For example, the cleansing of lepers depicts the removal of defilement from spiritual outcasts. The unstopping of deaf ears pictures the arousing of heedless hearts to hear God's truth. The stilling of the storm symbolizes the calming of the person terrorized by the adversities of life. The giving of sight to the blind portrays the giving of spiritual insight to sin-blinded souls.

Miracles have been termed "acted sermons," or "parables in concrete." Augustine said, "They have a tongue of their own. . . . All the acts of God are themselves words for us. They are not as pictures, merely to look at and admire, but as letters which we must seek to read and understand" (Alan Richardson, *The Miracle-Stories of the Gospels*, SCM Press Ltd., London, n.d., p. 58).

This book does not deal with present-day miracles but only with the lessons of Jesus' miracles for the present day.

With minor overlapping, the chapter order follows the chronological sequence in which the miracles occur in the Gospel record.

WHY
MIRACLES?

A schoolteacher was trying to convince a sixth-grader that what he had learned in Sunday School about Moses leading the Israelites through the Red Sea was no miracle. "It was nothing out of the ordinary," explained the skeptical teacher. "Actually, Moses and the Israelites simply walked across a two-inch-deep marsh called the Red Sea."

The bright sixth-grader responded, "Wow! Then the Lord really did save the day when He drowned the whole Egyptian army in a little puddle of water!"

Miracles—did they really happen?

The miracles of Jesus—did they actually occur?

His miracles, as are all biblical accounts, are related as factual events. Chapter after chapter, the Gospels record that by Christ's power numerous individuals—invalids, lepers, the deaf, blind, demon-possessed, and paralyzed—were healed of their illnesses. And in three cases the dead were restored to life. To deny these miracles reduces the authors of Scripture to unreliable witnesses and reporters, victims of superstition, or perpetrators of deliberate fraud, palming off their grandiose lies on succeeding generations. But most of Christ's miracles were performed before witnesses, many of whom were skeptical and unfriendly, and thus subjected to severe scrutiny. Yet these miracles were most firmly believed by the apostles. If we accept the testimony of the Gospel writers, we believe in the historicity of Jesus' miracles.

Jesus Is in a Class by Himself

As a doer of miracles, Jesus Christ stands head and shoulders above all others. No one has rivaled His plethora of marvels.

Do we hear of anyone today turning water into wine, stilling storms, walking on water, or feeding thousands with five loaves and two small fish? If such a person existed, his exploits would make headlines and be broadcast on the 6 P.M. news.

Likewise, *Jesus' healings were top-drawer, major, specific, dramatic, usually performed in full view of crowds.* A man born blind sees; a longtime paralytic walks; the skin of a victim of leprosy becomes clean; deranged people find their right mind; a withered hand turns normal; a speech impediment disappears; a severed ear is restored. No reports appear in the sacred record of vague, ill-defined problems such as stomach pains, backaches, or stiff necks, nor are X rays required for proof.

Also, Jesus' healings were instantaneous. The only exception was the blind man who first saw dimly, then clearly, in a two-step event. Many reported healings today are gradual, taking several days or even months, perhaps interrupted by relapses. Also, we refer to the healing of marriages or of relationships which, though commendable, fall short of the decisive, immediate feats reported in the Gospels. To mention gradual emotional or relational improvements in the same breath or category as Jesus' sudden, dramatic bodily cures seems both a contrast and an injustice to the power He demonstrated.

Moreover, Jesus had a 100-percent success rate. He healed all who were brought in contact with Him. Though He did not do many miracles in His hometown area because of unbelief, no instance is recorded of any sick person coming to Him and remaining ill. At sunset, after He had rebuked the fever of Peter's mother-in-law, "the people brought to Jesus all who had various kinds of sickness, and laying His hands on each one, He healed them" (Luke 4:40, NIV).

Those claiming the gift of healing today, if honest, must admit many failures. Says seminary professor Lewis B. Smedes: "One requirement of honesty in a public ministry of healing is full and accurate reporting, both to the faithful and to the world at large. The minister who engages in healing should publicize his or her failures as loudly as the successes. Chronicles of healings should include failed attempts to heal, prayers for healing that were answered in death, apparent healings of people who soon relapsed into the disease from which they were healed—all of this alongside of the grateful reports of success. Reports that ignore these and tell only of the successes are, we insist, disingenuous exercises in pious deception" (*Ministry and the Miraculous, A Case Study at Fuller Theological Seminary,* edited by Lewis B. Smedes, published 1987 by Fuller Theological Seminary). We expect golfers to report their bogeys as well as their birdies.

So, with a mere touch or with an authoritative command—not bothering with diagnosis, nor prescribing medical treatment, nor requiring a period of convalescence—Jesus healed the sick, the handicapped, and the demon-possessed. No other miracle worker has ever measured up to His prowess. He is the Super Miracle Worker—in a league all by Himself!

What was the purpose of these striking, sudden, and successful miracles? What lessons do they have for us today? What is Jesus Christ saying to the church of the twentieth century through His miracles of the first century?

Before we answer, we shall note the way skeptics try to explain away Jesus' miracles. Also we shall deal with the definition of a miracle, note the number and categories, and finally suggest what messages miracles of Jesus have for us today.

Miracles Denied

Rationalists use ingenious explanations to deny the miracles. To explain the healing of Peter's mother-in-law, they imply that her fever was slight and had just run its course. Also, the return of her son-in-law and the presence of their honored guest, Jesus, with His cheerful word and sympathetic touch, prompted her to sense her duty, thus rousing her to her feet. Yet Dr. Luke wrote that she was suddenly delivered from a "high fever" (Luke 4:38, NIV). Unless a genuine miracle, how did the event motivate "all the city" to gather at her door that same evening, bringing "all that were diseased" for healing? (Mark 1:32-33)

Unbelievers suggest that a leper had already improved to the extent that all Jesus did was to declare him clean—no cure, but merely the pronouncement of wellness. Yet Dr. Luke described him as "full of leprosy," which at Jesus' word "departed from him" (Luke 5:12-13). As a result, Jesus' fame spread far and wide, bringing great multitudes for healing (v. 15). Only a bonafide cure, not mere medical judgment, could explain such widespread impact.

To nullify the miracle of Jesus walking on water, scoffers say the episode likely took place in darkness when the disciples could not see clearly. Being closer to shore than they estimated, they mistakenly supposed Him walking on water when He was really stepping on land. But those seasoned sailors would not be easily deceived as to the distance from shore.

To unbelievers, the stilling of the storm on the Sea of Galilee was nothing more than Jesus' announcement in dramatic fashion that the storm would soon end. But if so, why did the disciples react with fear and remark among themselves, "What manner of man is this, that even the wind and the sea obey Him?" (Mark 4:41)

Antisupernaturalists who find a natural explanation for every Gospel miracle resemble the scholar who said, "When I meet an alleged miracle, I treat it as a legend." But such critics ignore the fact that the Gospel writers were eyewitnesses of these events. Further, since they were followers of Him whose name was the Truth, how unlikely they would be guilty of writing fiction.

Another strong reason for accepting Jesus' miracles as history is their close connection with His teachings. With the miracles so intertwined with the narrative, and so woven into the message, to reject the miracles is to tear away the very fabric of the entire record. Miracle and message hang or fall together.

For example, to deny the miracle of the feeding of the 5,000 is to render unintelligible certain consequences in the narrative. Only because the crowd saw the free lunches did they clamor to make Him king. His following discourse on the Bread of Life is contextually marooned, apart from the miracle of feeding.

Jesus opened the eyes of a blind man, then proclaimed Himself the Light of the world. Immediately before raising Lazarus, He declared, "I am the resurrection and the life." Much of His teaching regarding the Sabbath and the inconsistencies of Phariseeism arise out of healings He did on the Sabbath. If miracles are eliminated, the Gospel accounts become completely unreliable.

What Is a Miracle?

The word *miracle* is often used loosely. To many, the term is applied, for example, to such as Voyager II transmitting pictures of Neptune 2.7 billion miles to earth, viewing by TV a baseball game a thousand miles away, the safe landing of a plane whose flamed-out engines suddenly start up after the plane fell 19,000 feet over the Atlantic, remarkable answers to prayer, timely protection, and even the new birth. But our definition of *miracle* will be limited to a narrower sense.

Four words appear most frequently in the New Testament to denote miracles:

power—translated "miracle" nine times;

wonder—16 times, always used with "signs," something astonishing;

work—over a dozen times, mostly in John;

sign—about 60 times with the idea of signaling or signifying.

Using these four words, we define a miracle as an event performed in kindness through divine power, creating wonder, signifying the authenticity of the Lord's messenger. Three of these words appear together in the same verse several times in the New Testament, although not always in the same order. Jesus was "a man approved of God among you by miracles [powers] and wonders and signs, which God did by Him in the midst of you" (Acts 2:22).

● *Powers.* If someone escapes death in a bad auto accident, a friend will likely comment, "It was a miracle he wasn't killed." But for a happening to qualify as a miracle in the biblical sense, God would have to use supernatural power to interfere with the usual course of nature. The Greek word for power gives us our English word *dynamite.*

Because God is not a prisoner of His own natural laws (notwithstanding philosopher Hume's view to the contrary), He can choose to act apart from them. The owner of a complicated model railroad usually operated it from a control box, but on rare occasions he stepped midst the miniature tracks to pick up an engine or boxcar to reposition it. A miracle occurs when God steps into His universe and transcends the usual laws of nature to do something unusual. God, always present in sustaining, providential power, has chosen to work on that occasion in an unfamiliar style.

Whether we believe in miracles boils down to our concept of God. If we believe God is omnipotent, it isn't difficult to believe in miracles. As Paul asked, "Why should it be thought a thing incredible with you, that God should raise the dead?" (Acts 26:8) Since nature does not straitjacket God, He can use a higher force to overrule our lower order. Jesus' miracles evidence His power over demons, disease, nature, and death.

● *Wonders.* The exercise of this divine power produces a state of wonderment in the eyewitnesses. To qualify as a miracle in the narrower sense, the event must be palpable to the senses—most often sight. The extraordinary and sudden character of the event is observed and kept remembered. Therefore, the new birth does not fit this restricted definition because regeneration takes place within and is not observable by others at its occurrence. When the results of the inner born-again experience surface in the outer life, especially in a radical conversion, it will certainly be regarded as a miracle in the broad sense. Also healings of the emotions or of marriages would be considered miracles in the broad sense but not in the technically biblical definition with requires sudden, visible drama.

The Aztecs of Mexico speak of miracles as "long-necked things" because they cause people to stretch their necks to see something amazing. The display of Jesus' power in healing the palsied man amazed the people (Mark 2:12). After Jesus walked on the water, the disciples were "sore amazed" (6:51). At the huge catch of fish, Peter "was astonished, and all who were with him" (Luke 5:9). A miracle invariably elicited a feeling of awe, making the people wonder.

- *Works.* John frequently called miracles "works" (5:36; 7:21; 10:25). Jesus said, "Many good works have I showed you from My Father" (10:32). Interestingly, most of His miracles involved healing the sick and flowed out of His sympathy for suffering humanity.

Jesus did not perform any miracle for His own advantage. He turned water into wine to alleviate the embarrassment of the hosts at a wedding. On the other hand, He asked for a drink of water from a woman at the well. When dying, He was dependent on bystanders to ease His thirst. He fed thousands from a handful of bread and fish, yet would not change stones into bread to satisfy intense hunger caused by a 40-day fast. Though He raised the dead, He refused to lift a finger to save Himself from death.

Seven of Jesus' 35 miracles (a remarkable 20 percent) took place on the Sabbath: healing a demoniac (Mark 1:21ff), Peter's mother-in-law (Mark 1:29ff), an invalid (John 5:2ff), a man with a withered hand (Matt. 12:9ff), a man born blind (John 9:1ff), a woman crippled for 18 years (Luke 13:10ff), and a man with dropsy (Luke 14:1ff). Several of these miracles took place not only on the Sabbath but in a synagogue, incurring the wrath of religious leaders who would rather a person continue in illness than see some man-made law broken. But

THE MIRACLES OF JESUS

Jesus preferred the welfare of people above dead tradition and out of kindness healed on the Sabbath.

● *Signs.* Jesus' unique miracles were designed to do more than benefit mankind and produce amazement. They challenged the imagination and summoned viewers to open their eyes to spiritual truth. A close relationship existed between the marvelous deeds, and the person and mission of the performer. That's why the word "wonder" is never applied by itself to miracles, but instead appears in combination with "signs." "Signs" may appear alone, "powers" alone, or "works" alone, but never "wonders." It's always "signs and wonders" (e.g., John 4:48; Acts 7:46). Jesus' wonders authenticated Him as the divinely commissioned Messiah. His powers displayed the insignia of His Godhead. He urged His hearers to believe His oneness with the Father because of "the very works' sake" (John 14:11). John's stated purpose in choosing the miracles in his Gospel was to signal the deity of Jesus. He wrote, "Many other signs truly did Jesus in the presence of His disciples, which are not written in this book; but these are written that you might believe that Jesus is the Christ, the Son of God" (20:30-31).

Nicodemus was duly impressed by His marvels, saying, "We know that Thou art a teacher come from God, for no man can do these miracles that Thou doest, except God be with him" (3:2).

SURVEY OF THE MIRACLES

At the end of each line in this listing of miracles is a capital letter which identifies a category. N stands for nature, H for healing, and R for resurrection.

Miracle	Matthew	Mark	Luke	John	C
1. Water into wine				2:1-11	N
2. Nobleman's son				4:46-54	H
3. Catch of fish			5:1-11		N
4. Demon-possessed		1:23-28	4:33-37		H
5. Peter's in-law	8:14-15	1:29-34	4:38-39		H
6. Leper	8:2-4	1:40-45	5:12-14		H
7. Paralytic—roof	9:1-8	2:1-12	5:18-26		H
8. Lame—Bethesda				5:1-9	H
9. Withered hand	12:9-14	3:1-6	6:6-11		H
10. Centurion's servant	8:5-13		7:1-10		H
11. Widow of Nain's son raised			7:11-17		R
12. Blind, dumb, demoniac	12:22-23		11:14		H
13. Storm stilled	8:23-27	4:35-41	8:22-25		N
14. Gerasene demoniac	8:28-34	5:1-20	8:26-39		H
15. Jairus' daughter raised	9:18, 23-26	5:21-24, 35-43	8:40-42, 49-56		R
16. Woman with issue of blood	9:20-22	5:25-34	8:43-48		H
17. Two blind men	9:27-31				H
18. Dumb demoniac	9:32-34				H
19. 5,000 fed	14:13-21	6:30-44	9:10-17	6:1-14	N
20. Walk on water	14:22-33	6:45-52		6:15-21	N
21. Daughter of Canaanite woman	15:21-28	7:24-30			H

17

THE MIRACLES OF JESUS

Miracle	Matthew	Mark	Luke	John	C
22. Deaf man with speech problem		7:31-37			H
23. 4,000 fed	15:32-38	8:1-9			N
24. Blind man— second touch		8:22-26			H
25. Boy demoniac	17:14-21	9:14-29	9:37-43		H
26. Coin in fish's mouth	17:24-27				N
27. Man born blind				9:1-7	H
28. Lazarus raised				11:1-44	R
29. Woman crippled 18 years			13:10-13		H
30. Man with dropsy			14:1-6		H
31. Ten lepers			17:11-19		H
32. Two blind men, one Bartimaeus	20:29-34	10:46-52	18:35-43		H
33. Barren fig tree cursed	21:18-19	11:12-14 20-21			N
34. Malchus' ear			22:50-51		H
35. Catch of 153 fish				21:1-11	N

● *Their Number.* The list contains only the 35 specific miracles Jesus performed. Spread over a three-and-a-half-year ministry (42 months), Jesus' 35 miracles would average fewer than one a month. However, we know that in addition He healed countless other unnamed individuals. In a burst of hyperbole John ends his Gospel by declaring that if all of Jesus' works were recorded, "even the whole world would not have room for the books that would be written" (21:25, NIV). Though the miracles form a high percentage of the Gospel record (over 30 percent of Mark), the miracles are not disproportionately prominent. The authors do not use extravagance in their descriptions, but are objective and factual, even though reporting the same event with minor variations, and usually including the profound impression made on the spectators.

Examination of the listing shows Matthew reporting 20 miracles; Mark, 18; Luke, 20; and John, 8. Only one miracle occurs in all four Gospels: the feeding of the 5,000. Eleven appear in three Gospels, 10 in the Synoptic Gospels (Matthew, Mark, and Luke), also called the Triple Tradition, and 1 in Matthew, Mark, and John. Six are described in two Gospels only (3 in Matthew and Mark, 2 in Matthew and Luke, 1 in Mark and Luke). Seventeen are written in only one Gospel (3 in Matthew, 2 in Mark, 6 in Luke, and 6 in John).

● *Their Classification.* As previously mentioned, the miracles may be divided into three major categories: nature, healings, and resurrections.

The nine nature miracles are: turning water into wine, full catch of fish, stilling the storm, feeding the 5,000, walking on water, feeding the 4,000, coin in the fish's mouth, withering of the fig tree, and the postresurrection catch of 153 fish.

Three times Jesus raised the dead: the son of the widow of Nain, Jairus' daughter, and Lazarus.

Twenty-three times He healed.

Lessons for Today

Why did Jesus perform miracles? Certainly they were not given for us to duplicate. We are not called to walk on water, still storms, turn water into wine, feed thousands with a few loaves, or heal people born blind. Then what significance do they have for us today?

● *Miracles have an apologetic purpose—to authenticate Jesus' authority.* Miracles are not spread evenly through Scripture but are clustered around three critical periods of history: the Exodus years, the years of the struggle of the prophets against idolatry, and the years of Christ on earth. In each case the miracles authenticated servants of God. The miracles of the plagues and wilderness wanderings confirmed Moses and Aaron as divinely appointed leaders. The miracles performed by Elijah at Mt. Carmel and by his successor, Elisha, established their divine commission. The miracles in the Gospels verified Christ's heavenly mandate, showing that He is indeed the very Son of God, the assigned messenger from on High, who speaks for the Father and whose word is to be heard.

The miracles which continued into the apostolic period certified the apostles as messengers of Christ. However, miracles were the exception in Bible history. Centuries passed without any occurring. John the Baptist did no miracles (John 10:41), but when Jesus came on the scene, Nicodemus admitted to Him, "We know You are a teacher who has come from God. For no one could perform the miraculous signs You are doing if God were not with him" (John 3:2, NIV). Jesus pointed to His miracles as evidence of His divine commission (5:36; 10:25). Peter in his sermon at Pentecost declared, "God publicly endorsed Jesus of Nazareth by doing tremendous miracles through Him" (Acts 2:22, TLB).

The sign gifts were given for the difficult years of the infant church. Who would believe the word of these unlearned men with their fantastic story of One who rose from the dead? The apostolic leaders were not left unaccredited. Their performance of miracles authenticated them (2 Cor. 12:12). When the New Testament was completed, the need for such credentials diminished.

Some believe that on the frontiers of mission fields today, where the situation approximates that of the early church, and where missionaries need a power beyond their own to confront the forces of evil, God at times transcends some law of nature to show His authority over idols, to give remarkable answers to prayer, to protect His servants, and to punish scoffers.

It should be stated that the Lord performs miracles today. Though many purported miracles do not stand up under unbiased investigative procedures, yet many credible accounts by reliable witnesses of bonafide miracles do exist. However, it should also be said that it is the Lord who in His sovereignty chooses the place, the time, and the person.

● *Miracles have an evangelistic purpose—to awaken saving faith.* At the conclusion of his Gospel, John stated that his

20

purpose in recording certain miracles was not only to signal the deity of Jesus, but also to lead his readers to receive eternal life through faith in Him. He wrote, "But these are written that you might believe that Jesus is the Christ, the Son of God; and that believing you might have life through His name" (John 20:31). John's purpose was not only apologetic but also evangelistic.

The miracles became an essential part of apostolic preaching. Hearers were challenged to believe on Jesus because of His works. But the signs did not convince everybody. Many did not believe even after the feeding of the 5,000 or after the raising of Lazarus from the grave. Had not Jesus said, "Neither will they be persuaded, though one rose from the dead"? (Luke 16:31) The miracles possessed a double-edged character: they were signs, not proofs. Though they were not conclusive evidence of Jesus' messiahship, they did authenticate His claims and instructions for those who had ears to hear. Because of His miracles, many received Him as Saviour and came into possession of eternal life.

● *Miracles have a merciful purpose—to show Jesus' compassion.* Jesus never used His power capriciously, or for His own aggrandizement, or for the trivial, needless, or malevolent, but always to show kindness to the sick, the tormented, the hungry, the embarrassed, the fearful, the failures, the sorrowing, or to those with only one child. How often we are told that Jesus healed and helped because He was moved with compassion (e.g., Matt. 20:34; Mark 3:5; 6:34; 5:19; Luke 7:13). Not surprisingly, William Barclay titled his book on the miracles *And He Had Compassion on Them.*

Jesus' mercy on the sick has been a great inspiration to doctors, nurses, ambulance drivers, and medical researchers—those who care for the sick. Recently, World Vision began supplying prosthetic devices for some of the 60,000 Vietnamese who lost legs, arms, and hands at the time of the 1975 Communist takeover. World Vision President Robert Seiple finds the Gospel account of Jesus restoring a man's withered hand an apt metaphor of his organization's efforts: "We've been asked to restore the withered hand." Lewis B. Smedes suggests that the promise of Jesus that believers would do "greater works" than He (John 14:12) may be fulfilled in the total scope of healing in all the medical and psychiatric hospitals, sanatoriums, clinics, and other institutions that Christians have built and operated around the world. All told, Smedes suggests, they have probably brought about countless more healings than our Lord performed during His brief sojourn on earth (*ibid.*, p. 31).

● *Miracles have a prophetic purpose—to declare the ultimate triumph of God's kingdom over the forces of evil.* A war, fought in heaven in time past, resulted in rebellious Satan's expulsion from God's presence. Now an evil enemy of God, Satan exerts his perverse and malicious will on both man and his environment. With its storms and earthquakes, nature is unruly and out of kilter. The earth is infested with disease, plagues, and demonic influences. "The whole world is under the control of the evil one" (1 John 5:19, NIV).

Christ came to conquer Satan and bring in His own rule. All Gospels begin with the same announcement: namely, that the divine kingdom is at hand. The ministry of Jesus was a life-and-death war against forces that had seized control of the world. By defeating Satan on his own territory on a localized, limited scale, Jesus demonstrated His full, ultimate victory over the evil one. His miracles were announcements of the impending destruction of Satan's dominion. Though Satan's doom was delayed, it was sure. Someday the kingdoms of this world will become the kingdoms of our God and of His Christ.

Jesus said He had come to "preach deliverance to the captives, and recovering of sight to the blind, to set at liberty them that are bruised" (Luke 4:18). When He sent His disciples out, He gave them power over unclean spirits, and to heal all manner of sickness. When imprisoned John the Baptist wondered if Jesus were the promised Messiah, Jesus sent word to remind John that the lepers, lame, and deaf were healed, and that the dead were raised (Matt. 11:2-5). The working of miracles was a part of the proclamation of the kingdom of God by their attack on the enemies of God. All this was a foretaste of the total triumph of a coming age when Satan's forces would be subdued by the revelation of Jesus Christ, who with a cosmic cleanup would usher in a new heaven and a new earth where there would exist no pain, no sickness, no storms, no darkness, no hunger, no thirst, no demons, no death.

Lewis B. Smedes suggests that "the phrase 'signs and wonders' is biblical language for the revelatory events of a salvation history that had its climax in the incarnation, death, resurrection, and advent of the Spirit, leading to the birth of the Christian church. Therefore . . . we may best honor the unique acts of God in Jesus if we do not speak of answers to our prayers for healing as 'signs and wonders' " (*ibid.*, pp. 27-28). But Christ's great kingdom has not yet been ushered in. During the interim, the miracles have yet another significance for us.

● *Miracles have a pedagogical purpose—to symbolize redemptive truths.* As "acted parables," miracles illustrate how God deals with mankind in the matter of salvation. They emblematize the spiritual blessings God bestows on needy lives. They are specimens of God's redemptive activity—vehicles of instruction.

God uses variety in saving men. Jesus healed a variety of ills, such as demon-possession, blindness, deafness, paralysis, and hemorrhaging. Miracles occurred in a variety of places: in a house, on a lake, in a desert, by a grave, in a garden, in a synagogue, at a wedding, during a funeral procession. He healed in a variety of ways: by some physical act such as touching, spitting, applying clay, by having His garment touched, or by simply speaking a word. Sometimes He healed at a distance, or in the midst of a crowd, or after leading a victim out of the town, or by sending a person to a pool.

Similarly, God does not save people in stereotyped ways. Of course, everyone must come through Jesus Christ to the Father, but there are countless ways to Christ. The conversions in Acts took place in a variety of ways: in a chariot on a road, in a house, by a river, in a jail, at midnight, at noon; some occurred quietly, others dramatically.

According to his own later confession, when Benjamin Disraeli married the widow of his close friend, Mrs. Wyndham Lewis, he did not love her but married her for her money and social status. But in the following years she created such an atmosphere of tenderness that Disraeli, enchanted with her, fell deeply in love. On the other hand, while Disraeli was Prime Minister of England, Teddy Roosevelt, a student at Harvard, met Alice Hathaway Lee, who later became his wife. He said, "I first saw her on October 18, 1878 and loved her as soon as I saw her." Roosevelt fell in love suddenly, whereas with Disraeli love grew slowly. Likewise, some fall in love with Christ over a period of time, like Lydia, whose heart the Lord apparently opened gradually; others, with dramatic suddenness, as did Paul on the Damascus Road.

Jesus' cure of various diseases illustrates the multiple effects of His saving grace. The cleansing of the leper symbolizes the removal of defilement from spiritual outcasts. The raising of the paralyzed depicts the giving of strength to sinners to walk in paths of virtue. The curing of the deaf portrays the awakening of deadened perception. The healing of demoniacs shows that He can release entrapped sinners from the grasp of Satan. One preacher, considering the healing of the Canaanite woman's daughter a foreglimpse of the missionary character of the Gospel, titled his sermon, "The Promise of the Children's Bread to the Gentiles."

The variety of Christ's healing ministry typifies the fact that He is the Physician of the soul—not only the General Practitioner but also the Specialist who can successfully treat every species of deficiency and every problem. Perhaps these spiritual recoveries would also be part of the "greater works" Jesus said His followers would do. Calming the sea was important, but more remarkable is stilling the tempest that rages in the hearts of anxious souls! Feeding the 5,000 was amazing, but how much more beneficial to feed restless mankind the Bread of Life! Giving sight to a physically blind man was marvelous, but how much more exciting for a sin-blinded man to see spiritual truth! Thus, the miracles tell us not only what Jesus did then for man's physical well-being, but also what He still can do, and is still doing, to meet man's spiritual needs today.

● *Variety of persons who have faith.* Faith had a place in Jesus' miracles. *Sometimes it was the faith of the sick person*—for example, blind Bartimaeus who called out for mercy. Or the woman with the issue of blood who touched the hem of His garment. Healed, she heard Jesus say, "Daughter, be of good comfort; thy faith hath made thee whole" (Luke 8:48).

Sometimes it was the faith of those who brought the sick to Jesus, as in the story of the four men who carried the paralytic to the crowded house where Jesus was teaching and broke through the roof in order to let him down at the Healer's feet. Mark records that "when Jesus saw their faith," He performed a healing (2:5). It was also the faith of the Canaanite mother in behalf of her daughter that resulted in a miracle.

Then, in many cases, it was simply the faith of Jesus, motivated by the impulse of His own love, such as in the healing of the blind man in John 9. In the three raisings of the dead, the initiative lay with Jesus who exercised faith. Before raising Lazarus He prayed, "Father, I thank Thee that Thou hast heard Me" (John 11:41-42).

Sometimes faith was mustard-seed size, mingled with unbelief, or exercised from a distance. Since faith is required to bring a work of God into the lives of the spiritually ill, perhaps as we bring relatives and friends to Jesus with our faith, they may also come to faith in the Saviour.

● *Faith apart from miracles is superior to faith dependent on miracles.* To the nobleman who wanted his son healed, Jesus said, "Except ye see signs and wonders, ye will not believe" (John 4:48). While not condemning, Jesus mourned over this spiritual babyhood. Though belief because of miracles could lead to mature faith, the very act of seeking a sign contradicts that which pleases God—simple faith. Jesus said, "This is an evil generation; they seek a sign" (Luke 11:29). Jesus never reduced Himself to the level of a magician by performing a miracle merely to satisfy curiosity or to entertain. He knew faith based on miracles rested on a shaky foundation. Those who wished to make Jesus King after seeing Him miraculously provide free lunches later forsook Him when they began to understand His spiritual demands. Jesus' assessment of the worth of miracle-based faith compared to simple faith is shown in His comment to Thomas after showing him the marks in His hands and side: "Because thou hast seen Me, thou hast believed; blessed are they that have not seen, and yet have believed" (John 20:29).

● *Physical health not the most important matter.* Though Jesus healed all who came to Him, those He did heal ultimately fell sick again and died. Their miraculous healings were not permanent in this world.

How sad that people become more excited over wonders in the physical realm than workings in the spiritual domain. Meetings that deal with bodily healing often attract more than services that cultivate the soul. Preoccupation should not be with outward manifestations in preference to inner dealings. Reordered lives are more important than rearranged molecules.

Though disease may typify sin, it is not on the same level. Bodily health, indeed a major blessing, is not the *summum bonum,* nor is it vital as soul health. The kingdom of God and His righteousness are to be the chief objects of mankind. Though Jesus sympathized deeply with those burdened with illness, He did not teach that if only people were physically well, then all was well. Rather, He taught, in effect, "What shall it profit a man though he have perfect health, and lose his soul?"

One's soul will live on somewhere forever. What a tragedy to have sight restored only to go out into eternal darkness! What advantage to even be raised from the dead, then to again die and go out to a lost eternity, which is the case unless the soul has come into a right relationship with Jesus Christ! Spiritual deliverance is far more urgent and will bring at Christ's second coming the physical deliverance for which the entire creation longs (Rom. 8:18-23). If we seek first of all the growth of the soul, the body will at that coming day receive its health. Perhaps this sense of priority influenced such evangelists as Whitefield, Finney, Moody, and Sunday, not to encourage miraculous healing as a public element of their soul-winning crusades. Billy Graham is a current example.

Sometimes suffering is God's way to make us think on eternal matters. A wealthy but godless man who lived in a mansion was stricken with paralysis. Unable to follow the pursuits which had consumed all his energies, he turned to the things of God. They wheeled him into church where during testimony time, half raising himself in his chair, he would say, "I thank God for my dear paralysis. Otherwise I might never have known the Lord Jesus as my Saviour!" Someone said, "Pain is sometimes God's loudspeaker to rouse the deaf sinner to the greater pain which will be his should he keep on in his present way." Also, for the believer, suffering of the body may be God's way of refining the soul.

A relief worker in West Africa asked a national pastor what American Christians should pray for God to give African people. The pastor replied, "As important as food and water are for our people, they're only temporary. Pray that our Christian leaders may show our fellowmen that what they need for their eternal welfare is Jesus Christ, who is the Bread and Water of Life."

2

WATER
INTO WINE

During animated conversation at a dinner in Amsterdam there came a sudden hush. The silence was broken by a Dutchman remarking, "A minister walked by!" It was explained to an American visitor that whenever an awkward lull stops a good conversation, this remark is used to explain the sudden silence. The idea is that nothing could ruin the conviviality of a party faster than the presence of a clergyman.

But this was not true of Jesus during His earthly ministry. Karl Olsson puts it this way:

> He was, despite the sad world He inhabited and the solemn destiny which lay coiled in Him, the prime host and the prime guest of the party. He ate and drank; He let Himself be doused with perfume; He was concerned about wedding wine and wedding garments. Without denying anything that was sad or sinful, bloody or pallid, Jesus was indeed Lord of the Feast (*Come to the Party*, Word, 1972, p. 10).

Jesus was no party pooper. The traditional marriage ceremony mentions His "performing His very first miracle at a
wedding in Cana" where, to avoid the couple's embarrassment
at the depleted supply of beverage, He changed water into
wine. The story is told in John 2:1-11.

The Need
Very early in His ministry, Jesus and about six of His followers
arrived in Cana in Galilee, a little village where today stands a
church said to be the site of the miracle. An Egyptian apocryphal gospel says that Mary was a sister of the bridegroom's
mother. If so, this would explain Mary's interest in the wedding refreshments and the presence of Jesus. Since He had not
come to earth to rob humanity of its glad times, He accepted
the invitation.

Never yet in the 30 years of His life had Jesus performed a
miracle. The apocryphal gospels, excluded from the biblical
canon, depict Him in childhood performing absurd and inconse-
quential miracles, such as leaping from His mother's lap to
disperse threatening dragons, or making mud sparrows which
at the clap of His hands came to life and flew off. But John's
statement that changing water to wine was Jesus' first miracle
nullifies all such accounts.

● *No wine.* The wedding celebration with all its merriment
and honor was the grand event of life for the bridal pair. Wine,
as the symbol of exhilaration and joy, was an absolute essential
at the feast. Though the priest on duty and the Nazarite vower
had to refrain from partaking, all ordinary people drank wine.
"Without wine," went the Jewish saying, "there is no joy." So,
when the servants at this wedding saw the wine fast running
out, they were alarmed at this looming breakdown of hospital-
ity. The couple would never live down the shame.

Mary, seemingly involved in the wedding, recognized the
plight of this young couple. Unless something were done
quickly, social disaster threatened bride and groom. Perhaps
the added presence of several of Jesus' followers hastened the
shortage of drink and weighed a sense of responsibility on

Mary. So she turned to her son. "They have no wine." Her request, as well as sensing the couple's predicament, testified to her confidence in His power. No miracle of Christ was done to show off. Rather, His miracles were motivated by comparison and related to needs. Here Christ was asked to relieve the deep humiliation of bride and groom, a favor of no small value.

● *No wine of life.* The drama of the moment set the stage for a miracle with a deep lesson. The power of Christ to change water into wine signified His ability to bring joy into a life of boredom, frustration, emptiness, and gloom. The plea, "They have no wine," goes deeper than a lack of beverage at a wedding. It's the cry of a human heart without the joy of Christ. For the man apart from Christ, there inevitably comes a time when the wine runs out, and the joy, zest, and high of life disappear.

Novelist Ernest Hemingway seemingly had everything going for him, but eventually he put a shotgun to his head and killed himself. Actress Marilyn Monroe, despite her fame, wealth, and beauty, found that the wine of life had turned to bitter water, and also ended her life.

Not only do many non-Christians feel empty even with all their money, pleasures, and talent, but countless believers find their Christian life a dreary drudge. Worship has become a boring recitation of creeds and singing of hymns. Devotional study is nothing more than a storing up of dry, biblical facts and doctrinal concepts that lie like rotting fruit on a shelf of their minds. Their faith is burdensome, displaying a neurotic need to repeatedly ask forgiveness and make sure they have surrendered the key to every corner of their lives to the Master. Legalism demands wearying attendance at all church meetings, rigid periods of prayer, and a dutiful spirit which compels people to accept every church task that comes along. They are modern versions of medieval ascetics with their cold monasteries, hair shirts, self-flagellations, and debilitating diets. Life has long since lost its joy. Though they have no intention of ending it all, their wine has turned to water.

• *Eventually the wine runs out.* For the non-Christian, the wine sooner or later turns sour and then dwindles to drips and drops. If ever a person was qualified to pass judgment on the ability of earthly goods and glory to satisfy the human heart, it was King Solomon. He tried mirth, magnificent mansions, might, money, music, material possessions, and mistresses. He indulged in every pleasure and spared nothing to fill the emptiness of life (Ecc. 2:1-10). But his conclusion was, "Vanity of vanities . . . all is vanity" (1:2). Modern psychology would call it existential vacuum. It's really a matter of running out of wine.

The wine may fail early in life. Consider these facts: some 6,000 American high schoolers take their lives every year; 2 million more try to kill themselves; and another 6 million seriously consider it. Many men and women surrender to a midlife crisis. Suicide is not a stranger to old age. Natural delights have their place, but to depend on life's exhilarations leads to inevitable failure. Though surrounded by jovial companions and comfortable circumstances, the unbeliever discovers that earthly joy has given out and turned to hopelessness. But the revelation of one's own wretchedness may be the first step in turning to Christ, who can exchange the oil of His joy for our mourning, and who by satisfying the deepest longings of the human heart can put a song in our mouths.

• *The role of Mary.* Though Mary had never witnessed a miracle by her son, yet she had treasured in her heart all the wondrous words revolving around His virgin birth, the visits of the shepherds and wise men, the songs of Anna and Simeon, and His dialogue with the learned doctors in the temple at the age of 12. Probably a widow for many years, in emergencies she had repeatedly turned to Jesus as the head of their home in Nazareth. So now, with confidence in her son's ability to meet this crisis, she sent out her SOS, "They have no wine" (John 2:3).

Jesus' answer was a gentle rebuke. "Woman, what have I to do with thee?" By using the term *woman,* Jesus was not indulging in rudeness. He used the same word to her on the

31

cross, "Woman, behold thy son!" (19:26) If she were wishing Him to use this occasion to openly declare Himself as the Messiah by somehow providing the needed wine, He was replying, in effect, "Let Me do it My way. My hour has not yet come. Do not encroach on My Father's timetable."

Accepting the mild rebuke, with confident expectancy His mother said to the servants, "Whatsoever He saith unto you, do it" (2:5). This command would prepare them to receive and carry out a strange order from someone who was only a guest.

The Miracle

Standing nearby were six large stone water jugs used for purification purposes, enabling people to wash their hands before eating to be ceremonially clean. Water was also used by a host to wash the feet of guests, or to clean cups (Mark 7:3-4). Jesus ordered the servants to fill these jars with water, which they did, to the brim. This showed that the jars contained only water, and that nothing else could be added since they were full to the very top.

Then Jesus told the servants to carry the contents to the maître d' of the feast, who tasted it and declared its high caliber: "Thou hast kept the good wine until now." Not only was the wine of top quality, but it came in quantity too. Since each jar held two or three measures (a measure being the equivalent of 8½ gallons), each jar contained between 17 and 25 gallons. The six jugs had a total capacity of between 100 and 150 gallons. Counting a half pint to a glass, these vessels had enough for 1,600–2,400 servings, another example of the prodigality of God. In superabundance, Jesus satisfied the needs of those attending the feast. Jesus, who would not work a miracle in the wilderness to assuage His own hunger, here performed a miracle to provide ample beverage for the guests.

Though the maître d' at first attributed this good wine to the groom, the servants knew differently and doubtless soon informed the astonished guests of the real facts. "We poured in water, and then poured out wine! We did what Jesus told us to do." Jesus was exalted and the faith of His followers strengthened. John sums it up: "This beginning of miracles did Jesus in

Cana of Galilee, and manifested forth His glory; and His disciples believed on Him."

• *A real miracle.* In his autobiography, *Confessions of a Theologian,* Carl F.H. Henry tells how in his youth he learned from a Long Island magician to turn water into what looked like wine and then back again into what looked like water (Word, 1986, p. 37). Some would attribute the Cana miracle to a magician's trick.

Many other attempts have been made to explain away this miracle. Some scholars have suggested that the story was adopted from a tale of the wine-god Dionysius, whose temple on the island of Andros had a fountain of water which on his feast day, January 6, miraculously changed into wine.

Some put forth the notion that these jars had been previously filled with wine so that the residual wine sediment gave the water the flavor of wine.

Another claims that the guests just imagined in their semi-intoxicated state that the water had turned into wine.

Others allege that Jesus, wishing to make a present of wine, pretended it was water changed into wine. Having already freely indulged, the guests were easily persuaded to go along with this make-believe. Some hold that John, who recorded the event, was either in on the jest, or else shared the delusion in his semi-stupor. However, the narrative evidences no hint of haze or forgetfulness of details. Rather the writer vividly recalls the dialogue between Mary and Jesus, the exact number of waterpots and their specific capacity, the filling of them to the brim with water, and the comment of surprise by the master of the feast. The wine was provided in so remarkable a way as to produce on the minds of the disciples the indelible impression that a genuine wonder had taken place. They accepted it as history.

When a little later John returned to that area, he associated the town with the miracle. He wrote, "So Jesus came again into Cana of Galilee, where He made the water wine" (John 4:46).

If we cannot trust John as an accurate eyewitness of this

THE MIRACLES OF JESUS

miracle, how can we trust him when he reports other words
and deeds of the Saviour in the rest of his Gospel? The authenticity of the fourth Gospel is at stake.

● *Wine-drinking in the New Testament.* Invariably the mention of this incident raises the question of wine-drinking. Did
Jesus drink wine? Was it intoxicating? Does this episode encourage today's believers to drink wine? Admittedly, the problem of wine is not the point of this miracle, but here are some
brief observations.

(1) A candid reading of John 2:1-11 makes it impossible to
escape from the conviction that the wine here was more than
grape juice. It was called "the good wine." Jesus probably did
partake of the common wine of the day, but He was not a
"winebibber," as some of His enemies called Him.

(2) A clear distinction must be made between wine as we
know it today and the wine of Jesus' day. There is a similarity
and there is a difference. The wine of that era was intoxicating, but it was also mixed with water.

The ratio of water to wine varied, but on the average it was
three or four to one. When the ratio dropped to one to one,
such a mixture was termed "strong drink." A distinction is
often made in the Old Testament between "wine" and "strong
drink" (Lev. 10:9). Wine may have been understood to be a
mixture of wine and water, whereas strong drink was undilut-
ed wine. According to the Talmud, the normal mixture used at
the Passover was three parts water to one part wine.

(3) Though possible, it would not be easy to become intoxicated on the usual wine mixture. Robert H. Stein in a *Christianity Today* article, "Wine-Drinking in New Testament
Times" (from which many of the above-mentioned facts are
taken), says that "to consume the amount of alcohol that is in
two martinis by drinking wine containing three parts water to
one part wine, one would have to drink over 22 glasses. In
other words, it is possible to become intoxicated from wine
mixed with three parts of water, but one's drinking would
probably affect the bladder long before it affected the mind"
(June 20, 1975).

34

(4) The ordinary table beverage of the Mediterranean world in Roman times was wine mixed with water. Wine was used as a beverage because water was unsafe to drink. To boil water was tedious and costly. The easiest way to make water safe for drinking was to mix it with wine.

(5) The drinking of wine mixed with water in biblical times does not encourage wine-drinking today. If drinking unmixed wine, or even wine mixed one-to-one with water, was frowned on in ancient times, how much more disapproved would be the drinking of distilled spirits in our day in which the alcoholic content ranges from three to ten times greater.

We are all aware how alcohol use rages like a fire out of control. Alcohol is responsible for an estimated 25,000 traffic deaths annually. As the nation's number-one health problem, alcoholism costs the economy about $117 billion a year. An estimated 25 to 40 percent of people in general hospital beds are being treated for the complications of alcoholism. Someone quipped, "Liquor puts the quart before the hearse." The Christian who doesn't wish to be a stumbling block will think carefully before using the miracle of water into wine as justification for social drinking.

Joy, Jubilation, Exhilaration
● *In His initial miracle Jesus chose to deal in gladness, showing that He is the author of overflowing joy.* The night before the Crucifixion He said, "These things have I spoken unto you, that My joy might remain in you, and that your joy might be full" (John 15:11). Forbidden to get drunk with wine, believers are commanded to be Spirit-intoxicated, singing spiritual songs and making melody in their hearts to the Lord (Eph. 5:18-19).

John the Baptist was an ascetic, a quality which many mistakenly connect with Christianity. But Jesus was not stern and austere, but joyful and sociable. Because He came eating and drinking, He was found often at the dinner table. People enjoyed His company. Jesus did not come to rob people of their joy. Too easily people connect Christianity with black clothes and long faces. In his grim code for children at his school near

35

Bristol, England, John Wesley unwisely did not permit games, play, or observance of holidays. Jesus' first miracle corrects the false impression that sadness signals spirituality, and gloom indicates godliness. Though Jesus was no stranger to sorrow, the underlying tenor of His life was joy. He came that we might have joy in abundant measure. He turned water into wine, whereas too often His followers try to turn wine into water.

● *Jesus gives joy even in the common things of life.* He can turn the ordinary into the extraordinary. For believers, common joys take on deeper meaning and added zest. The wonders of the stars and of plant and animal life are seen as the handiwork of God. Before his conversion Jonathan Edwards was terrified of thunderstorms, but afterward as he watched the play of lightning and listened to the majestic voice of thunder he found "sweet contemplation of my great and glorious God."

When D.L. Moody came out of his rooming house the Sunday after his conversion, he thought the sun shone more brightly than ever before, and that the birds were singing to him. The Lord gives joy in simple things such as a baby's smile, health, food, and friends.

● *Jesus especially honored marriage.* John records seven pre-resurrection miracles of Jesus, beginning at a wedding and concluding with a grave from which He raised Lazarus, showing that He is Master of life from the altar to the tomb. He sanctified marriage by His presence at the wedding and by the performance of His initial miracle there. He didn't cast gloom over the marriage celebration or disapproval of the joy. He stamped as sacred the love of man and woman in matrimony. We are not surprised when He is referred to as the Bridegroom, and the church as His bride.

● *Jesus instituted a new dispensation.* Moses began his ministry in Egypt with a miracle of judgment, the plague that resulted in the water of the river Nile turning into blood.

Christ's miracle reversed this process, becoming a symbol of the contrast between the Old and New Testaments. Law and judgment came by Moses, but grace and forgiveness came by Christ. Christ is superior to the prophets, Moses, Aaron, and the old sacrificial system. The old ritual was dead, and the jars were now filled with the new life. The water of Jewish legalism had changed into the wine of salvation by grace.

● *Jesus can meet any emergency.* Though already believers, the disciples were strengthened by this miracle. If their Master could turn water into wine at will, then He had the power to solve any crisis they might ever meet. If they kept on following Him, He could take care of anything and everything.

● *Jesus can do exceedingly above our needs.* With the total quantity in the six jars amounting to between 100 and 150 gallons, enough for 1,600–2,400 servings of wine, it left a large supply for days or weeks to come. Since it is believed by some that six disciples accompanied Him, perhaps Jesus was paying His debt of gratitude by giving six waterpots full of wine as a wedding gift.

Surely He who supplies so generously in the physical realm will not be less lavish in the spiritual. His gifts are the best in quality and quantity. When He gives, He gives big. His peace passes understanding. His pleasures are forevermore. His joy is unspeakable and full of glory.

A skeptic said to a converted alcoholic, "Surely you don't believe those Bible miracles such as Christ changing water into wine." Said the Christian, recalling the poverty and squalor he had caused his family, "I've no difficulty in believing that story. Come to my home and I'll show you how Christ changed beer into carpets, chairs, and a piano!"

● *Jesus transforms our drudgery, griefs, failures, and boredom.* A time comes to all of us when we run out of wine. Drudgery is a part of living: cleaning the house, buying groceries, filling the car with gas, changing diapers, getting meals. In addition to the monotonies of life come disappointments and

37

grief. Like Mary, we should accept the situation, not run away from it. We may turn our stumbling blocks into stepping-stones. Instead of reacting bitterly and revengefully at troubles from which no one is promised exemption, we must look to the Lord to bring meaning out of pain. Joy may come through a mingling of grief and hope. We see the rainbow in the storm. We relinquish the pain to God and hold out our cup to let Him pour in the new wine of blessing.

Researchers at the 3M Company were trying to invent a new, stronger glue. Though the formula flopped, one of the researchers exclaimed, "But look at what it does!" The result—Post-it Note Pads, those little self-sticking yellow notes that can be attached to an item and be easily removed. From seeming failure came a financial success. Out of that Cana couple's embarrassment came their marvelous experience.

Sir Wilfred Grenfell, English medical missionary who labored in Labrador, visited Johns Hopkins Hospital in America to find a head nurse. Promising neither salary nor expenses, he made this offer: "If you want to have the time of your life, come with me and run a hospital next summer for the orphans of the Northlands." A nurse who accepted the offer later wrote, "I never knew before that life was good for anything but what one could get out of it. Now I know that the real fun lies in seeing how much one can put into life for others." New exhilaration put a kick in her life.

● *Jesus saves the best till last.* According to the custom of the day, the inferior wine was reserved till later in the feast so that the dulled senses could not discern its inferiority. But the maître d' at this wedding expressed surprise on tasting the high quality of this new wine, thinking that the groom had reversed the usual order, saving the best till last.

Satan and his world order do it the other way, serving the best first, then the worst later. The young drinker enjoys his liquor in those early years, but doesn't realize that at the last it "stingeth like an adder." Alcohol can turn a man of distinction into a derelict in the gutter. TV shows a story of illicit sex but doesn't show the frequent results of unwanted pregnancy, unwed motherhood, the temptation of abortion, or the contraction of AIDS.

Whereas Satan turns the good into bad, Jesus turns the bad into good. The pleasures of sin are enjoyed for a season, then comes the wages of sin—death. But in God's providence He brings good out of evil. He leads His people through the wilderness before bringing them into the Promised Land. First the cross, then the crown. He makes all things work together for His glory and our good. The path of the just shines brighter and brighter till the full light of day. Sorrow may last through the night but joy comes in the morning. The beggar Lazarus with his sores, rags, and hunger found himself in Abraham's bosom. The poet Browning quoted an old rabbi, "Grow old with me, the best is yet to be." Or as Lelia Morris' Gospel song says, "Jesus' love is sweeter . . . as the years go by."

The wedding in Cana reminds us of a wedding yet to be—the Marriage Supper of the Lamb. There Christ will be more than a guest; He will be the Bridegroom, and the church will be His bride. In His presence will be fullness of joy, and at His right hand pleasures forevermore. All who thirst are invited to come and buy wine and milk without money or price.

Human instrumentality. Jesus used instruments in bringing the wine to the guests. Though it was He who changed the water into wine, it was the servants who poured the water into the jars, then brought wine to the thirsty. Much as the disciples carried the miraculously multiplied loaves and fishes to the 5,000, so servants carried wine to the wedding guests at Cana. A major duty of believers as we pass through life is to bring the wine of divine joy to those who are troubled in heart.

Jack Eckerd in his 40s bought a couple of run-down drug stores in Florida. Fifteen years later he had the most profitable chain in the nation with 1,700 retail stores in 15 states and with more than $2.5 billion in sales. In an interview in *Decision* magazine (June 1988), he said: "I wasn't getting as much zest out of the business as I had before. I started looking for a new avenue. I got into politics and had a couple of interesting runs at the governorship and the U.S. Senate. I would think, 'Look at what you've got, old guy! What more could anyone want?' I'd answer, 'Nothing, but still I'm not happy.'"

Influenced by Charles Colson, Eckerd opened his heart to Christ and made Him Lord of his life and possessions. Today in his 70s, he directs a foundation that operates wilderness camps in five states for troubled youth. He also leads a private agency set up by the state of Florida to run its prison industries. Says Eckerd, "I have a deep peace that I never had before. That empty feeling has left. Jesus has put my life in perspective." Or perhaps we could sum up the change—water into wine.

OVERWHELMING CATCH
OF FISH

F ishing is fun! The front page of our local daily last winter
    carried the picture of a fisherman sitting on a sled on a
frozen lake near Bear Mountain in New York State. The cap-
tion read, "Hooked on Ice Fishing." The story told how fishermen cleared off the snow, drilled holes in the ice, then settled
down for a long, cold wait in the below-freezing temperature.
What brings a fisherman out of a warm bed before dawn to
brave a windy, frozen lakeshore? The article gave the fisherman's answer, "I like it. I don't miss a chance to fish all year
round." He had just caught a 22-inch pickerel!

Fishing has always been fun! So much so, that a well-known
preacher of an earlier generation on his way to his Sunday
morning service couldn't resist the temptation. Lyman Beecher, father of Harriet Beecher Stowe, who authored *Uncle
Tom's Cabin,* on his usual route was crossing a stream when a
big trout leaped into the air. Remembering that he had hidden
a rod and tackle under the bridge, the clergyman quickly
reached for his equipment. He landed the fish immediately.

THE MIRACLES OF JESUS

But without time to admire his lovely catch, he slipped it into the tail pocket of his ministerial coat where he usually carried a large handkerchief. Arriving almost late, he hurried into the pulpit. Some of his congregation wondered why he seemed a little breathless, his cheeks rosy, and tie rumpled. The reason was revealed to his wife a week later. The absentminded preacher, forgetting the fish, had hung his ministerial coat in its usual place in the closet. Next Sunday morning, when his wife opened the closet door to dutifully whisk off his Sunday apparel, the horrid smell of a week-old fish exposed the tale of her husband's escapade.

Strange that the preacher should have so easily forgotten his prize catch. Many fishermen, rather than return catchless, will go to almost any length to conceal their failure, even composing unbelievable whoppers of how the big one got away. How well I recall a comic strip in which a man boasted of catching a fish bigger than a house. To prove it, the next frame showed the fish towering over a house which looked so small compared to the fish. But the final frame gave him away. He had taken a picture of the fish in front of his little daughter's dollhouse.

Not surprisingly, some thoughtful people ask, "Do all fishermen lie, or do only liars fish?" Seventeenth-century writer Isaac Walton dedicated his book, *Compleat Angler,* which went through five editions, "To the reader of the discourse, but especially to the Honest Angler."

In the early days of Christianity when believers were suffering persecution, they used the sign of the fish as a secret emblem of their faith. They frequently inscribed the symbol on the walls of the catacombs in Rome, and today it is sometimes seen on bumper stickers or worn as a pendant. According to *Unger's Bible Dictionary,* the five letters of the Greek word for fish stand for: Jesus, Christ, of God, Son, Saviour. It's also an appropriate symbol since it ties in with Jesus and His disciples, at least four being fishermen. Jesus Himself in one parable likened the kingdom to a net which caught many kinds of fish. Both miraculous feedings of the 5,000 and of the 4,000 involved fish. Jesus paid a tax for Himself and Peter with a coin

42

found in a fish's mouth. Twice the Lord gave His disciples huge catches of fish after fruitless nights of toil.

The Master Fishermen

Jesus' purpose in performing the miracle of the enormous catch of fish in Luke 5:1-11 was to do some fishing Himself. The four fishermen for whom He provided this enormous catch had not yet become His full-time followers. The first chapter of John's Gospel records the initial meeting of Andrew, John, and Peter with Jesus (1:40-42). Precisely when James met Jesus we're not told. But for months after their conversion these four alternated between traveling with Jesus and fishing. Though they spent considerable time in the company of Jesus, they still devoted blocks of time to their fishing business. As part-time followers, these four fishermen had observed Jesus in action in several well-known incidents, such as the miracle of turning water into wine, the chasing of the money changers from the temple, the healing of the nobleman's son, and the conversion of the Samaritan woman. The winning of many Samaritans through her testimony gave a little preview of the massive "fishing" assignment Jesus had planned for these fishermen in the yet-to-be-given Great Commission.

But Jesus knew that if they were to fulfill their worldwide evangelization assignment, He would need to intensify their training. So Jesus now was about to call them into full-time ministry. The Master Fisherman wanted to inspire these fishermen with enthusiasm for their future vocation—fishing for Jesus. Though they had come to know something of His power and teaching, they had not yet left all to follow Him. So He was about to perform a miracle that would persuade them to take this decisive step of full commitment. He wanted them to become His constant companions.

● *His use of the familiar.* The Master Teacher always took things at hand to explain things remote, the familiar to elucidate the unfamiliar. Boats, sea, fish, and nets were things that Peter, James, John, and Andrew knew best of all. So Jesus came to their level. Had they been men of the rod and staff, He might have spoken of lambs and sheep and shepherds. Had they been traders, He might have talked of shekels and profits. Had they been scribes, He might have conversed on books and quills. Had they been soldiers, He might have dealt in spears and swords. To the magi-astronomers of the East, He gave a star. To the woman who came to the well for water, He offered the Water of life. So in this event He spoke in terms these fishermen could understand through a miraculous action that was far more impressive than any spoken message.

The Miracle

Though Matthew, Mark, and Luke all relate the Lord's call to the four fishermen to a full-time assignment as Jesus' followers, only Luke reports the miracle of the fish leading to the call. It was early morning on the Sea of Galilee, called Gennesaret only in Luke 5:1, a body of water roughly 7 x 13 miles and nearly 700 feet below sea level. Its shores, dotted with prosperous towns and villages, were awakening to the hum of activity as the waters rippled under the early morning breeze. Fishing was the area's main industry.

Peter, Andrew, James, and John, two sets of brothers and partners in business, had been out all night but had caught nothing. Suddenly around a bend in the shore came a crowd, following Jesus, wanting to hear this unusual teacher. As crowd pressure built, Jesus spotted two empty boats from which the four fishermen had stepped to tend their nets. Commandeering Peter's boat, Jesus asked Peter to thrust the boat out a little from the land, so He could more conveniently teach the growing multitude. This was not the first time Jesus had taught from ship to shore. Though a larger audience could be reached, it was not an ideal teaching situation. How well I recall, at a summer youth camp, standing in a bobbing boat near a shore where teenagers were sprawled to hear my evening devotional. I was swayed, even if my congregation wasn't!

Though Jesus was fishing for men and women in that vast crowd, now He turned to a special target. Finishing His sermon, He asked Peter to launch out into the deep and let down his nets for a catch. Typically, Peter reacted between doubt and faith. "Master, we have toiled all the night, and have taken nothing" (Luke 5:5). As if to say, "We're experienced fishermen. You're a carpenter. The Sea of Galilee is our bailiwick. What do You know about this lake and fishing? If we haven't caught anything during the night, how likely are we to catch anything now in the daylight? It's really no use. We just finished washing our nets. And You want us to soil them again, and for no reason. Such poor timing." Then Peter added, hedging, "Nevertheless at Thy word I will let down the nets."

● *Peter's surprise.* Peter was joined by another, probably Andrew, in letting down the nets (5:6). Then came the shocker. They caught such a multitude of fish that their nets were about to break. Muscles bulged as they struggled. They signaled their partners, James and John, for help. As the two sets of brothers piled the silver cargo into the boats, both boats began to sink.

The miracle dazzled Peter. Some have tried to tone down the miracle by saying that Jesus, becoming aware of a shoal of fish, suddenly observing it moving out in the depths beyond the boat, merely gave directions to the fishermen as to where to cast their nets. But that wasn't the way Peter saw it. It was no mere accident with a school of fish just happening to be there, but the supernatural power of a Person who could control both the movements of the fish and steer them on any course He chose. Peter recognized Jesus as the cause of this extraordinary and unexpected success. So convincing was the event to Peter that it put an end to his earthly calling.

Jesus was proving His power over nature. At the Fall in the Garden of Eden came the curse on the ground with its thorns and thistles, requiring painful and sweaty toil to successfully till the earth. Paul wrote that the entire creation groans in travail, waiting for its liberation from bondage (Rom. 8:19-21). To demonstrate that He will one day ultimately bring about the redemption of creation, Jesus performed nine nature miracles. (See the list in chapter 1.)

45

Peter witnessed not only Jesus' power over nature but His control over the very part with which Peter was so familiar, the sea and the fish. Fish do not eagerly leap from the sea into nets at the order of someone standing on shore. "No one but the Creator could have made these fish act like this," thought Peter. He began to realize that he was in the presence of the Promised One. "This is the area in which I'm supposed to be the expert. But Jesus knows more about my occupation than I do! The fish in my lake are subject to Him. He's no mere mortal!"

Though Peter had known Jesus for some months, the supernatural glory of His real person now dawned on his heart. Peter saw his own sinfulness as he felt the tug of the breaking nets and the slow sinking of the overloaded boat. Falling before Jesus, he cried, "Depart from me, for I am a sinful man, O Lord" (Luke 5:8). The Lord answered, "Fear not" (5:10), then extended a great summons.

The Call to Be Fishers of Men

With Peter fallen at His feet, deeply overwhelmed by the huge catch, the Master issued this command, "Follow Me, and I will make you fishers of men" (Matt. 4:19; see also Mark 1:17). Luke puts it, "Henceforth thou shalt catch men" (5:10). Jesus invited all four men to leave their usual occupation and join Him in a new calling. Now instead of fishing for fish, they would fish for men.

Herein lies a major difference between their former employment and their new ministry. In fishing for fish, they brought death to that which had been alive. In catching people, they brought spiritual life to those who had been dead in sin. What a thrill to see people come alive in Christ. A man who wore a golden hook on his lapel was asked if he really was a fisherman. "Yes," he answered, then added, "but I fish for people."

When a little boy asked, "What's the biggest fish you ever caught?" he replied, "Two hundred and forty pounds, but I'd rather catch them your size." Then he gently led the lad to trust Christ as his Saviour.

● *Immediate response.* Obedience was immediate. Peter, Andrew, James, and John left nets, boats, business, parents, and all, and followed Jesus. Many of the strategies used in their old job would prove helpful in their new task.

Similarities in Catching Fish and Catching People

● *Cultivate a desire for fishing: feel concern for souls.* Just as many let fishing get into their blood, sending them out evenings and weekends to sit long hours on a wharf or in a boat, waiting for a nibble, so we need to develop a desire and patience to win people to Christ.

Too easily we forget that, even if he or she wears fashionable clothes, has a strong physique, a fat wallet, and a beautiful home, every person outside of Christ is headed for a lost eternity. A teenage girl said to a visiting missionary, "None of my family has ever talked to me about Jesus. Aren't they concerned that I'm lost?" Cultists shame many true believers with their zeal that sends them door-to-door, even in the worst of weather.

● *Go where fish are: have contacts.* Smart fishermen know about fish—their habits and habitats, unlike Simple Simon in the nursery rhyme who fished for a whale in a bucket of water. We must go where lost individuals are, even if it means organizing house-to-house visitation.

One preacher suggested that what many pastors are doing is merely exchanging fish (transfer of members). One pastor takes some fish out of his own bowl and drops them into the bowl of a neighboring pastor, who in turn gives the first pastor some other fish back, making each of them a keeper of the aquarium instead of a fisher of men.

Thus we need to have non-Christian contacts. When a pastor urged his congregation to invite unsaved friends to a crusade, several couples were shocked to discover they had no non-Christian friends to invite. What good is the salt if it never gets out of the saltshaker?

We are to be separated, not isolated. Perhaps we could get involved in a secular group such as the PTA or a service club.

THE MIRACLES OF JESUS

A Christian golfer I know tries to play mainly with unbelieving friends. We might invite a non-Christian friend to a sporting event. Someone said, "It's hard to convince a person you want to meet in heaven, if you don't want him in your living room."

● *Use discretion: be tactful.* An experienced fisherman keeps out of sight. He doesn't splash noisily into a fishing area and scare off the fish. Someone quipped, "Let the trout see the fishermen and the fishermen will see no trout." The Christian fisherman must engage in self-effacement if he is to catch people.

Fishermen must take care to keep their lines untangled. Overinvolvement in the affairs of life can divert our attention from the business of fishing for people. Failure to practice what we preach will also undermine the credibility of our witness. The student who tries to win a classmate to Christ, then cheats on an exam, will be unconvincing.

Witless witness turns off the non-Christian. Incredibly, one man let his dog run loose so that when neighbors phoned to complain he could give them the plan of salvation. However, we must never become so tactful that we never speak. A proverb puts it, "Silence is golden; sometimes it's yellow." A happy medium avoids coming on too strong and holding off in paralyzing timidity. When a near-blind washerwoman was seen witnessing to a storefront wooden Indian, bystanders laughed at her mistake. She replied, "I like the way I do it better than the way you don't."

● *Know your bait: know what to say.* A sign in a small town read, "Flies with which to catch fish in our locality." Here was a guaranteed, time-tested bait. The soul-winning fisherman may use different types of bait: a Gospel tract, a small-group Bible class, a kind deed, an invitation to a service, a book, a Sunday School paper. Paul, a great fisherman, followed this strategy: "I became all things to all men." To effectively fish for people we must be adaptable in our approach.

Surely we should learn the general steps in leading a person to Christ, such as those taught by Evangelism Explosion, The

Navigators, or Campus Crusade for Christ in its "Four Spiritual Laws." An outline need not be slavishly followed but may be adjusted to varying circumstances. It's wise to memorize Bible verses which substantiate the way of salvation, as well as those which refute the leading excuses given for rejecting the Gospel. We should always be ready to give an answer for our Christian position (see 1 Peter 3:15).

● *Know when to pull in the line: be alert for response signals.* The true fisherman is sensitive to any faint bite on his line. A hymnwriter told of entertaining a class of girls in her home every week during a summer vacation for an hour's singing, during which she told what had prompted her to write some of her hymns. She sometimes walked with girls afterward toward the avenue, chatting words of encouragement. A few years later she sat by the bedside of one of these girls who was dying; the girl told how eagerly she had been seeking the Lord at the time of these singing classes. Too shy to speak first, she never told her teacher. She said she used to linger every week, hoping against hope that her teacher would just say one little word that might be the messenger of peace, instead of the general remarks about hymns. Years went by before God chose other means to win her.

How often her words ring in the teacher's ears, "I ought to have been yours," meaning, "I should have been won by you. I should have been your fish, caught through your witnessing."

● *Exercise patience: don't give up.* Fishermen must be persistent, often waiting patiently for a nibble. Fishers of men "must not strive but be gentle unto all men, apt to teach, patient, in meekness instructing those that oppose themselves, if God peradventure will give them repentance to the acknowledging of the truth" (2 Tim. 2:25).

Though our witness seems unproductive, we should not become discouraged. A new church member testified, "Two years ago on my first visit to this church I chose one of your prominent members and, unknown to him, observed him closely in his business, social, family, and church life. After subjecting him to microscopic scrutiny for 24 months, I became convinced of the genuineness of his faith, and received Christ as my Saviour."

There is indeed joy at catching fish and people. A man on his first fishing trip in northern California landed a large silverside salmon after an exciting 55 minutes of playing him on his lightweight tackle. As he was congratulating himself on his fine haul, an officious-looking character came along and found out this was his first salmon. "That fish is going to cost you a lot of money," he said. The fisherman thought he had broken some law until the visitor explained, "Now you'll be coming up here every year for the rest of your life." The visitor was right. The sheer delight of such fishing cost him a tidy sum for annual return trips.

I'll never forget my teenage elation at catching my first fish, a puny perch pulled from Lake Ontario. I have seen students at Moody Bible Institute, Chicago, arriving back at school after an assignment on which they had won their first convert. Their joy was boundless.

The Coin in the Fish's Mouth

Peter, Andrew, James, and John left behind a comfortable existence to follow their Master who had no apparent income or a place to lay His head. They likely wondered, "How will we be fed? How will our families exist? Who will pay the bills, such as our taxes?" Perhaps to remind these disciples that He was fully capable of meeting their needs, Jesus performed another miracle that involved the catching of a fish.

When a collector from the temple internal revenue service at Capernaum asked Peter if his Master paid tax, Jesus told Peter, in effect, that as Sovereign over all, He did not need to pay, but so as not to offend, added, "Go thou to the sea, and cast an hook, and take up the fish that first cometh up and when thou hast opened his mouth, thou shalt find a piece of money; that take, and give unto them for Me and thee" (Matt. 17:27).

Dr. Willard M. Aldrich, founder of Multnomah School of the

Bible, Portland, Oregon, in an article in the school's paper, relates that while he was meditating on how easy it was for Jesus to send Peter to the sea and get a tax payment out of the fish's mouth, he suddenly realized that the miracle of God's provision—the fish's mouth—was the story of his life (*Multnomah Messenger,* Vol. 7, No. 1, Winter 1988). Dr. Aldrich recounts incident after incident of God's wonderful provision for needs through the years: study at Wheaton College and Dallas Theological Seminary, free rail travel as the son of a Northern Pacific Railroad engineer, marriage to a wonderful wife and keeping food on the table for nine children, purchasing a farm on a down payment with a gift of $500. His final episode concerns building a two-story addition to the farmhouse for his growing family. He reports: "We built the addition, prayed, and carefully watched the mail for the arrival of our miracle. This went on until we began to doubt our decision to trust God for our need. Just about the time we had nearly made all the theological adjustments to account for unanswered prayer, a letter arrived from an unfamiliar woman with a Pittsburgh address, sending a check for $5,000. Another coin from the fish's mouth."

Another Miraculous Catch of Fish

Still another episode reinforced their Master's summons to take men alive. Back in Galilee in that 40-day period between the Resurrection and the Ascension, Peter, ever the leader, said, "I go a fishing" (John 21:3). Going fishing did not mean that he was giving up his discipleship and going back to his old trade. The Master had told the disciples to go into Galilee where they would see Him again (Matt. 28:10). But since they did not know how long it would be before He would appear, Peter proposed temporary resumption of their former craft till new orders came.

On that overnight expedition something happened to remind them of the miracle two years before. Again, after a night of fruitless toil, catching absolutely nothing, the Master appeared on shore and directed them to an immense haul of 153 fish. In this graphically described incident, He wanted them to understand that apart from Him their future ministry would be a failure. Only His power could bring results. The Lord didn't reprimand the disciples for fishing but did remind them that they had other business, success for which could come only from Him.

Becoming Fishers of Men

Peter's greatest fishing expedition took place at Pentecost when, along with the other apostles, he landed 3,000 souls. Most likely at the end of that day Peter and his fishing companions thought back to the time Jesus gave them a net-breaking load of fish and called them to be fishers of men.

Through the centuries Christ has been calling His fishermen to take men and women alive for Him. In the mid '40s a drunken derelict named Joe Killigrew stumbled into the doorway of New York City's Jerry McAuley Cremorne Mission on 42nd Street to get out of the rain. A few days later he received Christ. Two years later on the anniversary of his conversion, marvelously saved and delivered from drink, he was made superintendent of the mission. Several times my wife and I had dinner with him in his apartment over the mission. When Joe died in 1955, a speaker at his funeral estimated that in seven short years, because of his familiarity with the haunts and habits of neighborhood derelicts, this modern fisher of men had won more than 9,000 souls to Christ.

Most of us will never win people in large numbers like Joe Killigrew, Peter, Paul, Finney, Spurgeon, Moody, Billy Sunday, or Billy Graham. Most, like Andrew, will catch men one by one. Though our Lord influenced the crowds, He devoted much time to people individually. To Him a single soul was a great audience. On nearly 20 different occasions, He dealt with only one person. He seemed to use the line more often than the net. For example, He won the woman at the well, Zaccheus, and the dying thief, all on a one-to-one basis. Even Jesus wasn't always successful, as in the case of the rich young ruler.

Many churches have "Fishers of Men" clubs aimed at winning people to Christ. Probably one of the most effective soul-winning groups reaching into out-of-the-way places is the Salvation Army. Lt. Colonel Lyell Rader tells of early one Sunday in New York City praying, "Lord, this is a big city. Certainly out of the millions, there's someone who needs to know the joy of salvation. I don't care if he went to bed plastered drunk at 5 o'clock in the morning. You can wake him up. You can shake him out of bed, and You can get him down here in time for our meeting."

It so happened that a man named John Martin, the manager of Hotel Algonquin, was lying in bed not far away. He had gone to bed at 5 o'clock that morning, plastered drunk. Waking up and unable to go back to sleep, he thumbed through the *New York Times*. On the church page he saw a tiny ad about a Salvation Army meeting that morning. Discarding that section, he turned to another part of the paper. He saw the same ad. With an oath, he tossed that section aside. The third time he saw the ad he said to himself, "You've seen Times Square every hour of the night. How about Sunday morning? I think there's a good bar down there right beside this Salvation Army place." So Martin dressed and went down to Times Square.

About this time Rader was telling his coworkers at their prayer meeting how he had prayed earlier. Someone repeated his request, "Lord, we don't care if the man went to bed at 5 o'clock in the morning plastered drunk. We ask You to touch him now." At that moment Martin was next door, looking into the bar. The Salvation Army loudspeaker was broadcasting the prayer meeting into the street. He heard the prayer continue, "You can wake him up. You can shake him out of bed, and You can bring him down here." Martin wondered if they were going to call out his name!

Unnerved by all this, he slipped into the meeting. After the closing prayer, Rader talked with him for four hours. Martin received Christ, and in weeks and months grew in grace by leaps and bounds. He eventually became the secretary of the Salvation Army corps and served faithfully.

Jesus Christ, the miracle worker and Head of the College of Fishermen, is still inviting people to become fishers of men and women.

A LEPER
CLEANSED

S ome years ago I became acquainted with a man from India as we drove on a short trip from a western suburb into Chicago to a denominational convention. His name was Davidas and he told me that when he was 16 he had become a victim of leprosy and spent five years in a leprosarium. When doctors pronounced him clean, Davidas returned home, married a girl, who, though never a victim of the disease, had been born to leprous parents. Some years later the disease recurred, forcing Davidas back to the leper colony. After a few years the disease was again arrested. For several years he had been living a normal life, and was then, along with his wife, operating a home for orphan boys in India. As president of India's Evangelical Baptist Association, Davidas was visiting the United States to attend his denomination's 15th anniversary celebration.

I must confess to a little apprehension that day on learning that my fellow rider was once a leper. But recalling that this disease is only mildly communicable reduced my anxiety level considerably. However, just the thought of leprosy makes many people shudder. Most of us have seen pictures of lepers with their ugly deformities, know they have been treated as outcasts for generations, and unconsciously dread contact with them. Millions still suffer from leprosy. Although the bacillus was discovered in 1874 by a Norwegian scientist, Dr. Gerhard Hansen (giving it the name of Hansen's disease or HD), all attempts to eliminate leprosy have so far proven unsuccessful.

A few years after I met Davidas, my wife and I visited the Kothara Leprosy Hospital in central India where he had spent several years. Never shall we forget arriving late one afternoon and receiving a cordial greeting from 400 lepers sitting on the ground in front of us. They sang songs and a few made speeches, then placed wreaths of flowers around our necks.

These lepers were not the most beautiful sight. Many had gnarled fingers. A little boy pathetically extended a hand which looked like a claw. One man had held a very respectable position as customs inspector for the Indian government. On his arrival at the hospital, he could not close either of his eyes, both hands were like claws, and both feet were paralyzed. The doctor in charge had operated on both eyes of this former customs inspector, as well as on his hands and feet. The patient showed us how he could now blink his eyes, straighten his fingers, and walk with a shuffle. Improvement, though slow during his two years there, was steady and definite.

Though chronologically, changing water into wine was Jesus' initial wonder, the first recorded miracle in the New Testament concerns a leper (Matt. 8:2-4, Mark 1:40-45, and Luke 5:12-16).

A Man "Full of Leprosy"

One day a leper came near Jesus. Doctor Luke describes him as "full of leprosy." Covered with sores, he was a repulsive sight. No wonder Matthew and Luke say, "Behold." Perhaps too, Jesus and the disciples were surprised at his sudden appearance.

At the start of the disease, a victim notices discolored patches on his skin, on which nodules later form, turning from

55

pink to brown. His skin thickens. Nodules gather in the folds of the cheek, nose, and forehead, making his face look inhuman. In time these nodules ulcerate, producing a foul discharge. Eyebrows fall out. The voice becomes hoarse and the breath wheezy. Hands often become bleeding stumps, as do the feet, making it impossible for the victim to wear shoes. Because of its slow progress, leprosy has been called "the remorseless nibblings of an unhurried death." Some lepers who came to the Kothara Leprosy Colony were covered with putrifying sores. This type is called Lazarian leprosy because it is surmised that the beggar Lazarus, who sat at the rich man's gate with sores covering his body, had this kind of leprosy.

The leper who crossed Jesus' path must have been a ghastly sight! Perhaps the disciples dropped back in horror at this grotesquely disfigured "ghost."

● *Leprosy: a type of sin.* Though the Bible nowhere declares it, biblical expositors generally regard leprosy as a type of sin. Leviticus 13 is devoted to a lengthy diagnosis of leprosy. Because a person diagnosed with leprosy was described as ceremonially unclean, the pollution associated with the disease suggests the defilement of sin. The next chapter, Leviticus 14, deals with the recovery from leprosy, which is never called healing but cleansing, a term which suggests removal of sin. Leprosy was often considered divine punishment for personal sin, as in the cases of Miriam, Gehazi, and Uzziah. The cleansing of the leper by Jesus in His first recorded miracle symbolizes the cleansing of a soul from the defilement of sin.

● *Leprosy: slow and insidious.* At a party in Calcutta, India, where guests were the rich, titled, and cultured, a lovely young woman danced with a Scottish doctor. Escorting her to a seat after a waltz, he asked, "May I have a word with you privately? I hope you won't take offense, but I couldn't help but notice a spot on your shoulder. Has it been there long?" The girl replied, "Yes, Doctor, several months, and I'm worried about it." The doctor arranged an appointment with a specialist for the next day. The verdict—leprosy. One little spot, but the disease was working insidiously within, and in time would spread gradually but surely, marring and scarring that beautiful body.

Like leprosy, sin begins in a small way and spreads insidiously, infecting all of one's faculties, twisting one's intellect, perverting one's emotions, hardening one's conscience, and enslaving one's will. Coveting leads to stealing. A little flirtation leads to adultery. A little anger grows into rage, perhaps murder. "They won't miss me," said a church member, sleeping in one Sunday morning. Then a month later he missed another church service, then more frequently till he was no longer attending.

● *Leprosy: insensitive.* Sometimes the advance of leprosy attacks the nerve centers, causing the affected area to lose all sensation. Suffering no pain when pain should be present, the victim has no warning of dangerous situations. He burns his hand severely without feeling anything. Before new buildings were erected at Kothara Leprosy Colony, patients' quarters consisted of mud huts. Rats came out of the walls at night and ate off the toes of sleeping leprosy patients who had no sense of feeling in these members. Eventually, cats were brought to rid the areas of rats.

Sin paralyzes and removes sensitivity to sin in its various forms. It becomes easy for the sinner to lie, cheat, and even murder without guilty feelings.

● *Leprosy: often caught from parents.* Contrary to public perception, leprosy is not a highly communicable disease. How then do people get it? Most cases occur in childhood, usually before the age of 15, apparently from long and frequent contact with afflicted parents. This makes it imperative to separate babies from parents who have leprosy.

Though leprosy is not inherited, a sinful nature is. Because we are the descendents of Adam, every child is born into this world with a sinful nature, which will soon express itself in sinful thoughts, sinful words, and sinful deeds. Every child is contaminated with the loathsome disease of sin passed on from

THE MIRACLES OF JESUS

our original parents. Paul wrote, "By one man's disobedience" many were made sinners" (Rom. 5:19).

● *Leprosy: isolating.* One of the tragic chapters in man's inhumanity to man has been the ostracism and even persecution of lepers. Though in ancient times many nations did not banish lepers, as in the case of Naaman, a leprous captain of the Syrian army (2 Kings 5), the Old Testament ordered the isolation of lepers. Diagnosis by the priest meant banishment from society. The leper had to live outside the camp, with his upper lip covered, crying "Unclean, unclean" (Lev. 13:45-46). Along with the ravages of physical breakdown, a leper had to suffer the disgrace of living as an outcast.

At the time of Jesus, a leper could not enter the temple or walk into Jerusalem or any walled city without suffering the penalty of 40 stripes. Allowed in the village synagogue, a leper had to be first to come and last to leave, and while there he or she was confined to an isolated chamber. The victim could never go home, nor engage in any business, but had to live off husks.

In the Middle Ages, lepers were forced to wear gray garments, to carry a bell or clapper to warn any nearby person of his presence, and to step off the road to let others pass. Victims were forbidden to bathe or wash their clothes in the rivers, and never permitted to enter public buildings. Some churches had a peephole so the leper could look in on the church services. In Canterbury, England, the Old Church of St. Martin's still has a little opening in the wall called the Leper's Squint.

Today children are often taken from leprous parents at birth, perhaps never to see them again. In some countries lepers tell no one of their illness, lest they be put in prison or killed. In China and India, lepers have been burned alive. In Burma they have been driven out to starve. As recently as 1967, 10 lepers were killed in South Korea when they refused to move out of a settlement near a village 50 miles west of Pusan.

Like leprosy, sin isolates. It separated Adam and Eve from

the Garden of Eden, sending them outside, as cherubim, with a flaming sword guarded the tree of life (Gen. 3:24). Sin drove Cain as a fugitive into the wilderness (4:14). Sin puts prisoners behind bars and will divide families in eternity.

Larry Ward, founder of Food for the Hungry and earlier with World Vision, once wrote in a *World Vision* magazine about a little, lone pine tree and a small bench outside a leprosy hospital on an island in Japan's Inland Sea. The tree was called "Good-bye Tree," for on the nearby bench incoming patients had to say good-bye to their loved ones. If only that "Good-bye Tree" could talk, what stories it could tell! Young lovers parting, vowing to be true. Aged couples parting and both of them about to walk alone after years of walking together. Parents whispering farewell to frightened children, wishing desperately they could take their place. Every good-bye here is for a minimum of 2 or 3 years, perhaps for life.

A lone figure limped to the bench, an elderly woman wearing a plain blue dress, a patient at the leprosarium. She sat down and, with hands folded in her lap, looked out over the waters of the inland sea. What was she thinking about? The long-ago day when her family said good-bye to her by this tree? Perhaps she was trying to imagine what they were doing now, those loved ones far away in the freedom of bodies not marked with her disease. Or perhaps she was wishing that by some magic she could reach out across the waters and tenderly touch a little grandchild, smooth a little boy's hair, or stroke a little girl's face. Another patient here wrote these lines:

Today I walked along the beach
Where no one else would be
And took my grandchild's picture from my breast,
And wept where none could see.

● *Leprosy: a victim is treated as dead.* It was better to be dead than to be a leper. A victim's isolation and dress proclaimed him a living corpse to be shunned by the healthy. When Miriam was afflicted with leprosy, Aaron begged that she be not considered as "one dead" (Num. 12:12).

Leprosy was a living death. Jewish historian Josephus de-

THE MIRACLES OF JESUS

clared that lepers were treated "as if they were, in effect, dead men." Sometimes in the Middle Ages, when a man learned he was a leper, the priest in gown and with crucifix led the man into the church and read the burial service over him.

In his Epistle to the Ephesians, Paul clearly states that those who have not yet trusted Christ as Saviour are "dead in sins" (2:1, 5). Mankind stands in need of divine life.

● *Leprosy: universal.* Leprosy is not a tropical disease but is found in most countries of the world. *Pulse,* published by the Evangelical Missions Information Service (12/6/85, vol. 20, no. 23), reports: "There are 15 million leprosy victims in the world, mostly in Asia, and the number is increasing. . . . The disease has built up a resistance to dapsone, until recently the only treatment available." Some believe that the disease was brought to the Western world, including Palestine, by the army of Alexander the Great on its return from India in 325 B.C. It was first brought to Britain by Roman soldiers who had served in Syria. Robert Bruce, King of Scotland in the 14th century, is believed to have been a leper.

A notable flare-up of leprosy occurred in Norway a century ago, and cases exist today in Scandinavian countries. Africa has millions of lepers; India has more than a million and a half; Korea, two million. World Vision's Korean Skin Clinic has treated some 20,000 lepers over the past 26 years. Many nations make no attempt to count their lepers. One African chief, afraid of giving his domain a bad name, listed only four, though everyone knew there were hundreds around.

Perhaps surprisingly, about 6,000 leprosy patients live in the United States; of the 1,600 who reside in California, 90 percent are refugees or immigrants from Southeast Asia and Mexico.

Though the majority of cases do occur within the tropics or subtropics, leprosy knows no bounds geographically, socially, racially, or culturally. Though relatively few in the world are lepers, and thankfully so, every person born into this world, except for Jesus Christ, is born a sinner. Sin knows no national bounds. Sinners abound in every nation under the sun. Every last one of us is a *moral leper in need of cleansing.*

When Yehiel Dinur, a concentration camp survivor who testified against Nazi Adolph Eichmann in 1961 at the Nuremberg
trials, walked into the courtroom and saw Eichmann for the
first time since the Nazi had sent him to Auschwitz 18 years
before, he stopped short, began to sob uncontrollably, and
then fainted in a heap on the floor. Mike Wallace on TV's "60
Minutes" once asked Dinur what happened. Was he overcome
by fear or hatred? On the contrary, Dinur explained that seeing Eichmann there, not dressed godlike in high-ranking army
garb, made him realize that the Nazi was just an ordinary man.
Commented Dinur, "I became afraid about myself. I saw that I
too was capable of doing what he did. I am . . . exactly like
him." But aren't we all moral lepers?

So leprosy is a suitable symbol of sin. Like leprosy, sin
turns out loathsome, though it begins with a small start and
works silently and slowly. Sin separates and destroys sensitivity, ultimately causing death. A leper in a leprosy colony in
Africa told this story:

> My home village is far away from here—nearly 200
> miles. In our tribe we have a man who is called the
> "Cleanser of the Village." He goes from village to village
> seeking those who are lepers. When he finds a leper, he
> places a rope around the leper's neck and leads him out of
> the village. He leads him till he finds a tree that is defi-
> nitely leaning in one direction. Then he ties the leper on
> the downward side of the tree and proceeds to chop
> down the tree. As it falls, it kills the leper. Then the
> Cleanser goes back to the village. He marches up and
> down and is given money and gifts because he has
> cleansed the village.
>
> When I found out that I was a leper, I knew that the
> Cleanser would soon get me. I ran away to the Leprosar-
> ium here where I have received help for my disease. I
> have also learned to be a mechanic and am now in charge
> of the diesel plants which run the station generators. I
> escaped the Cleanser of the Village and found friends who

cleansed me of my disease. I also became acquainted with the only One who could cleanse my soul.

Along Came Jesus

In South America a superstition says that if a leper gives his illness to seven others, he will be free of the disease. In India a superstition says that if a leper can induce a cobra to bite him, he will be cured. In Spain a superstition persists that if a leper could be touched by a monarch, the disease will go. Lepers who came across Jesus' path wanted to be touched by a monarch, the King of kings and Lord of lords.

That the leper under discussion ever came to Jesus is astonishing. Normally he would never have tried to approach an ordinary rabbi, for he would have been immediately repulsed. Under usual circumstances he would have accepted the inevitability of a lingering death. But when he heard of Jesus, who went about doing wonderful deeds like Elisha of old, perhaps this leper reasoned, "Naaman went to Elisha, so why shouldn't I go to this Jesus of Nazareth?" So he came, knelt, then fell prostrate at the feet of Jesus. Likely some of the crowd scattered at this point.

The leper beseeched Jesus, "If Thou wilt, Thou canst make me clean." He had heard enough about Jesus to know that He could heal, but not enough to be sure that He would. Might Jesus shrink from him like the others? But Jesus, moved with compassion, literally churning down deep inside over the plight of this tragic figure, said, "I will; be thou clean."

As Jesus spoke, He reached out and touched the untouchable. Touch and voice synchronized. Whereas most people of that day would have been repulsed by the leper, perhaps picking up stones to throw at him, Jesus not only had compassion but made physical contact, an unthinkable gesture which must have strengthened the leper's faith. For the first time since being afflicted with leprosy, the victim felt sympathy and love. Someone understood the agony of his outcast situation and the constant horror of his defiled condition.

Dave Roever, on river patrol in Vietnam when a phosphorus grenade exploded six inches from his right ear, suffered third degree burns over 40 percent of his upper body. Part of his right cheek was blown away. His gums were charred. His teeth were black. His right nostril was gone. Lacking an eyelid, his eyeball protruded grotesquely. As he lay recovering, he wondered how his young wife, Brenda, would react to his disfigurement.

When Brenda walked into the hospital room, Dave thought her more beautiful than ever. She stepped straight to his bed. Without the slightest sign of shock or repulsion, she bent down and kissed Dave on the left side of his face. Looking into his good eye, she smiled and said, "Welcome home, Davey, I love you." As she straightened up after the kiss, bits of dead skin hung from her lips. Dave thought of Christ who put on our dead flesh and smiled at us in agony from the cross (*Decision*, January 1988).

To the leper, Jesus' touch made all the difference. According to the law, Jesus should have become defiled. But instead of becoming unclean Himself, He brought cleansing to the leper. Despite his defilement, the leper was in contact with divine holiness. And he was well. The cure was immediate.

This man wasn't the only leper healed through Jesus' ministry. He empowered His disciples to cleanse lepers (Matt. 10:8). Jesus sent word to John the Baptist that His cleansing of lepers was a proof of His messiahship (11:5). Once He healed 10 lepers simultaneously. He dined in the home of ex-leper Simon (26:6). His cleansing of a few lepers around Palestine was a foretaste of His power to cleanse moral lepers of their iniquities.

Jesus ordered the cleansed leper, "See thou tell no man . . . show thyself to the priest, and offer the gift that Moses commanded, for a testimony unto them" (8:4). The leper would still need to follow the ritual prescribed in Leviticus 14 for a recovered leper. Telling people would create crowds that would hamper Jesus' ministry. But the ex-leper "began to publish it much, and to blaze abroad the matter," preventing Jesus from openly entering the city (Mark 1:45). Who can blame him when we think what his remarkable cure from such a loathsome disease must have meant to him. No

THE MIRACLES OF JESUS

such prohibition exists today to keep us from sharing with others what God has done for us. We are to unashamedly confess Christ before others.

Doubtless the ex-leper eventually saw the priest. Not often did priests see lepers healed. However, this phenomenon would begin to occur more frequently during the ministry of Jesus. By comparing notes, priests soon became aware that lepers were being cleansed by the power of a man named Jesus. Perhaps this was one more factor that explains why later "a great company of the priests were obedient to the faith" (Acts 6:7).

Wouldn't you think that anyone cleansed of leprosy would out of sheer gratitude say thanks to the one who healed him? Yet one day after ten lepers had cried out to Jesus for mercy and were cleansed, only one bothered to return and fall on his face to express gratitude. He had just felt new life suddenly pulsating through his body. Looking down, he had exclaimed in effect, "My fingers, my toes, they're like they used to be. Now I can go anywhere. But first I must go back to Jesus" (see Luke 17:11-19).

Jesus knew exactly how many He had healed, so He asked, "Where are the nine?" Before their cure their desperate condition drove them toward Jesus. After their cure they needed Him less than before, so they thought. The very miracle designed to lead them to Him accomplished their undoing. Why go back to Him? How tragic when we accept God's gifts but neglect the Giver.

Why didn't they return? One may have answered, "I wanted to be with my family, embrace my wife, and take my children on my lap." Another, "I had to get back to my business. I'd been gone so long." Whatever the reason, they were not maliciously ungrateful. But only the one who returned heard Jesus say, "Arise, go thy way; thy faith hath made thee whole" (v. 19). Ten were physically cleansed but only one spiritually healed. No matter how close our quest for Jesus has brought us, unless we personally bow before Him in adoring gratitude, our spiritual status is in question.

A modern leper wrote this letter from Greece:

64

Yes, I have the dreadful disease of leprosy. Yet I praise God for four things. (1) Clinical workers of the American Mission to the Greeks discovered my leprosy during house-to-house visitation. (2) I am thankful because AMG is giving me free a new multiple drug. Since my condition was discovered early, I should be healed in three years. (3) I am thankful for the people who donate money to AMG, making the new multiple drug free to leprosy victims. (4) I am thankful that I contracted leprosy because now I am regularly taught the Word of God and am thrilled about the gift of salvation which God gives to all who believe in Jesus who died on Calvary for us. Yes, I have much to be thankful for.

Identification with the Unlovely

Likely most of us will never have contact with leprosy patients, but another scourge—AIDS—is rapidly stalking the earth. Though for some the illness may come as a penalty for violating God's physical laws, others will be innocent victims. Just as leprosy is not highly contagious, neither is AIDS to those not in intimate contact. But through unbased fear, people ostracize AIDS victims today, just as they did lepers in Jesus' day. One victim confessed that the disease had plunged his spirit to the depths of despair, lamenting, "There were times when I thought no one would ever want to touch me or hug me again." Like Jesus, we must stretch our hands to the outcasts, distasteful as it may seem.

Some of the finest missionary biographies concern those who devoted their lives to lepers, but most moving of all may be that of a Belgian priest, Joseph Damien, who worked in the South Sea Islands. At 33, he was challenged by his bishop who needed someone to go to the leper island of Molokai, where lepers were abandoned to their terrible fate without comfort. Damien volunteered to spend the rest of his life in unpleasant exile.

He found the lepers a pitiable, hideous sight: faces with ugly holes where eyes had been, rotting mouths, ears often swollen many times their size, hands without fingers, feet merely stumps, and covered with open, revolting sores. Damien fought back the temptation to vomit or faint. He found the life of lepers no better than that of animals. For 16 years he lived among them, washing their wounds, holding their maggot-infested limbs, changing their bandages, sharing his plate of food. He built them better houses, a better church building, and a better water supply. He buried their dead, personally digging more than 2,000 graves, and conducted a funeral almost every day.

One day, spilling some boiling water on his foot and feeling no pain, he realized that he too was a leper. That day in the little Lepers' Chapel where he preached so often, he began, not with "My brothers," but with "My fellow lepers." He worked as death slowly ate away his body and he died hideously misshapen on Palm Sunday 1889. With two priests and sisters of charity kneeling at his side, one asked, "Will you, like Elijah, leave me your mantle?" Damien smiled, saying, "What would you do with my mantle? It is full of leprosy."

Once asked in a letter how he could do what he did, he wrote back, "As for me, I make myself a leper to gain all to Jesus Christ."

A PARALYTIC WALKS

Growing up on a Kansas farm, tomboy Venita Schlotfeldt rode horses, milked cows, and drove tractors. A college graduate and in her first year of marriage, she was severely injured in an auto accident caused by a drunken driver. As she lay on a cold, rocky roadside in Colorado, she thought she was dying. A few days later a doctor revealed to her that her neck was broken and that she would never walk again. After she spent six months in a hospital and received physical therapy, the doctors dismissed her, telling her husband, Larry, that she would never be able to take care of herself, or sit up for long, or have children. Advised by a relative to institutionalize his wife, Larry answered, "My place is with Venita. I love her and I'm staying with her."

Decision magazine (March 1987) details Larry's painstaking efforts to get his wife out of bed to sit in a wheelchair without her blacking out. When she could sit for a few hours, they began attending church again, enjoying the support of fellow believers. One day her doctor told her she was expecting a child. "I've never had a quadriplegic deliver a baby," he said. "I can hardly wait." Their child, a daughter, is now in her 20s.

Larry cut a gate in the side of the bassinet so Venita could slide her baby in and out. He made a table to fit on her wheelchair so she could dress the infant, which often took two hours because her fingers and arms were so weak. But lifting her baby out of the bassinet and working with buttons, snaps, and pins increased the strength of her back and fingers.

Two years later a son was born. When he was less than a year old, Venita read in their church magazine about the need for a handyman in Venezuela on a short-term basis. She knew her husband, who taught Spanish, had a desire to travel to a Spanish-speaking country, and showed him the article. Larry called for information. Learning that most missionaries had small children and that a wheelchair would be no problem, they went for the summer. In 1973 they returned as full-time missionaries, spending some wonderful years there. Their third child, another boy, was born in Caracas in 1975.

Now back in Minnesota, Venita often wishes she could go bicycling with her teenagers or walk beside her husband, but she prays, "Please keep me grateful. Help me remember where I was and how far You have brought me."

If we are amazed at the remarkable progress this determined woman has made over long years, no wonder people were astonished at the power of Jesus when in an instant He caused the paralyzed to walk. Venita, as the *Decision* article title suggests, progressed to become a "Missionary in a Wheelchair." But one paralytic whom Jesus healed took up his bed and walked off with it.

Remarkable advances have been made at the National Center for Rehabilitation Engineering at Wright State University near Dayton, Ohio. Eight of 35 paraplegic or quadriplegic people in a special program are walking through the use of electrical stimulation and braces. According to an Associated Press article, this program made headlines in 1982 when a woman walked a few halting steps while tethered to a large harness and even larger computer. With equipment now refined, this patient walks two miles a day.

The program has received wide recognition, including four appearances on "60 Minutes" and a TV movie. But think what news it would be if from among the more than half-million paralyzed in our country, a quadriplegic should suddenly rise from his bed or wheelchair to full, immediate use of his arms and legs. Yet on more than one occasion Jesus made a paralytic walk.

The Plight of the Paralytic
Jesus lived in four places: Bethlehem as a baby, Egypt as a refugee, Nazareth for most of His earthly life, then Capernaum, which became His base of operations as He began His ministry (Matt. 4:13). Though Jesus eventually engaged in missions to neighboring areas, His early Galilean teaching and wonders centered around Capernaum. Returning one day to "His own city" (Matt. 9:1), He healed a paralytic, a miracle recorded in three Gospels (Matt. 9:1-8; Mark 2:1-12; Luke 5:17-26).

Paralysis, whether partial or total, is devastating. Imagine having to be carried or pushed wherever you went. No self-propelling wheelchairs existed in Jesus' days. The victim was totally dependent on others to get anywhere. Even if he had wanted to join the crowd following Jesus, he could not have done so by himself. The paralytic represents the human race; in our own strength we are unable to walk the path Jesus wants us to tread. Spiritually paralyzed, we cannot rise up and steadily walk the road of righteousness.

The paralytic was quite confined. In our unregenerate condition all members of the human race are limited. We are rather like the big brown bear in Germany which most of its life had been locked up in a cage. All day long it would pace out the tiny space of its awful prison, 12 feet forward, then 12 feet back. The water the bear drank was stagnant slop, and its food was rotten garbage. Cruel people tossed cigarette butts into the bear's path to burn the pads of its feet and halt its march. But the bear plodded on, 12 feet forward and 12 feet back.

One day the famous Heidelberg Zoo bought this bear. Here bears did not live in 12-foot cages but had the run of plush grass with trees to climb, pools of clear water, the best of food, and other bears for company. However, when they opened the door to freedom, the big bear just kept on walking inside his cage, 12 feet forward and 12 feet back. Zoo workers had to scare the bear out. Outside his small cage now with almost unlimited space, he again began to pace the same distance, 12 feet forward, 12 feet back. Had they released him in a vast prairie wilderness, he undoubtedly would have acted in the same manner.

The paralytic in the Bible account was a captive of a limited space, a type of the human race, all of whom are prisoners in need of release from bondage. Commentator Charles R. Erdman suggests: "The disease from which the man suffered was far more serious than what is commonly known as 'paralysis'; it was rather like epilepsy. The control of the muscles was lost; but there were sudden paroxysms of pain, when the sufferer would fall, writhing in helpless agony; the attacks became more frequent, and relief was found only in death" (*The Gospel of Mark,* Westminster Press, Philadelphia, 1927, p. 44). The story indicates this paralytic could not walk. Erdman adds that he "was suffering from a still more terrible malady of sin, of which this disease was the startling symbol, and probably the result" (*Ibid.,* pp. 44–45).

The Four

A riddle asks, "What has eight ears and sings?" The answer—a quartet. We have male quartets, female quartets, and mixed quartets, but here was a quartet banded together (Mark 2:3), not for music but for helping a needy person. These four men were interested in one man. Too often we think in abstract of the lost in our community and fail to think in concrete terms of that spiritually paralyzed individual next door. Failing to be specific, we accomplish little. But these four men concentrated on one person.

Usually, it takes several faithful people to win one individual to Christ, though sometimes someone comes to Christ solely through one person. In my case, my two parents, two Sunday School teachers, my pastor, and an evangelist were all used in bringing me to Christ. As a boy, under sin's domination, I was influenced by six persons. One sows, one waters, one cultivates, one reaps; but because of the several, God gives the increase.

Perhaps it had been a fivesome before the paralytic had become ill. The four were deeply concerned over their pal, so crippled he couldn't walk anywhere with them anymore.

● *The four had faith.* We are told later that it was "when Jesus saw their faith" that He acted in behalf of the sick man (Mark 2:5). Time and time again Jesus healed because of the faith of someone who placed a needy person before Him. True, it is one's own personal faith that saves, but often it's another who first has the faith to believe that a friend will come to believe. Sometimes we must pray for others before they will pray for themselves.

These four had undoubtedly heard of the healing of Peter's mother-in-law and of the many healed at dusk at Peter's door; perhaps they had even witnessed one of the many miracles performed in the Capernaum area. Sold on Jesus, they thought, "Why can't He do it for our paralyzed pal? If we can somehow just get him to Jesus, He'll make him well!" So they devised a plan to put feet to their faith. They decided to carry the paralytic on his bedroll, one on each corner, right to Jesus. What if one of them had said, "Sorry, but tonight I've tickets to a play"? Or another, "I've put in a hard day at work. His weight will be too much for me. I'm entitled to take it easy." What if the Canaanite mother had been too busy to plead with Jesus for her demon-possessed girl? A man paralyzed for 38 years, waiting for a cure at the pool of Bethesda, told Jesus, "I have no man, when the water is troubled, to put me into the pool" (John 5:7). Are some of our friends crying out in their hearts, "No man cares for my soul"?

● *The four acted ingeniously.* This healing stands prominent among Jesus' miracles because of faith's ingenuity. It was a tough physical task to carry this man on a cot, even a short distance. When the men did arrive at the house where Jesus

71

was teaching, probably Peter's, they faced a problem. Not only was the place crowded inside, but the doorway was jammed. When Mark says that the four men could not get near Jesus because of "the press," he wasn't referring to reporters from the *Capernaum Courier* or the *Jerusalem Journal* but to the multitude mobbing the entrance. But this didn't deter the four. They were resourceful and daring. They did not say, "Well, it must not be the Lord's will." They had to find a way.

With the doorway crowded and windows too small, they thought of the roof. Palestinian houses had flat roofs used for many purposes, like storing things, drying flax, or meditation. Most had an outside stair up to the roof. Since lumber was scarce, beams were sparingly used for roofing, and the spaces filled with close-packed branches and reeds, then covered over with soil. To get to the roof would not be hard, nor would it be difficult to remove the filling between two of the beams and lower the cot through. The damage could easily be repaired. A common way of getting coffins in and out of small houses was through the roof. The four men reasoned, "If not through the door, then through the roof." The idea was inconvenient, unconventional, and unorthodox, but they meant business. We have a responsibility to bring our friends to the Lord Jesus despite obstacles.

Think of the incident from the standpoint of those under the roof. As the crowd listened to Jesus' teaching, suddenly they heard a pounding of feet above, then the sound of digging through the roof as the four men began to carve out a hole. It undoubtedly caused concern as pieces of the roof fell onto the crowd. Everyone looked up, some irritated at the disturbance. Likely, Jesus stopped, then resumed teaching. Suddenly a section of the ceiling gave way, dumping dirt, splinters, and reeds below. A man's fist showed through the roof, then eight clenched hands tore at the stuffing. Helpless, the crowd stood by, unable to comprehend what was happening. The opening grew larger till long and wide enough to permit a cot with the sick man on it to be lowered by ropes and positioned before Jesus.

These four friends had certainly put feet to their faith. God doesn't use angels to bring people to Jesus. Nor does the Bible ever command sinners to go to church, but it does order the church to go to sinners. It borders on blasphemy to pray for the salvation of a friend and then do nothing about it. Dr. R.A. Torrey said, "No prayer is sincere unless we do our utmost to get our prayer answered," obviously meaning if it is within our power to act. Perhaps the paralyzed man lived near Peter's house but no one had taken him there earlier when Jesus had healed so many from the city. Multitudes live within the shadow of Gospel-preaching churches who might be won if faithful, concerned Christians approached them directly. This paralytic had no legs of his own, but that day he had eight extra legs. As has often been said, "Christ has no feet but our feet to do His work today."

The Authority of Jesus
With debris falling all around and the cot coming to rest in front of Him, Jesus stopped speaking. It's hard to speak when the roof is caving in. Besides, the frail man at His feet looked up imploringly. Above, four perspiring faces peered through the hole in the roof. Noting "their faith," Jesus spoke.

● *Four or five?* When the Gospel accounts say that Jesus acted in response to "their" faith, did that include the faith of the paralytic, or only of the four men who carried him? Chrysostom believed it included that of the sick man. Some go so far as to suggest that the victim engineered the whole operation. Yet on the other hand, many think that faith was limited at the start to the four friends who carried him to Jesus, possibly against his will. Since the paralytic was seemingly passive throughout the whole episode, apparently never saying a word, he likely did not oppose their action. Perhaps, though, he had reached a stage of deep pessimism.

Responding to the collective faith of the four, and seeing a need deeper than the man's paralysis, Jesus declared, "Son [child], thy sins be forgiven thee." This was no mere desire or hope or prayer on the part of Jesus for the man's forgiveness, but a definite declaration of a fact already accomplished. His

73

sins had been forgiven. This statement raised the hackles of scribes sitting there, who reasoned, "Why doth this man thus speak blasphemies? Who can forgive sins but God only?" This assertion must also have astonished the crowd and surprised the four friends seeking his healing, not his forgiveness.

● *A connection between sickness and sin.* If a person suffers an illness, is it always because of some sin in his life? Sometimes illness may be traced to Satan's oppression (Luke 13:16; Acts 10:38). But in John's Gospel account (9:1-12) Jesus refuted the disciples' implication that the man was born blind because of either his own or his parents' sin. So, sickness does not necessarily mean sin in one's life. To teach such doctrine is cruel. But on some occasions an illness may be the result of personal iniquity. Possibly the man lowered from the roof was afflicted as an effect of his own misconduct. But the account does not mention it. If his illness was a result of sin, we are not told what the sin was. Jesus was too sensitive to expose it publicly. If the paralytic regarded his illness as a product of his misbehavior, Jesus knew his guilt hung as a heavier burden than the loss of his bodily health. The declaration of forgiveness provided a prelude to his cure, paving the way for Jesus' next statement.

A holistic approach to medicine recognizes the beneficial influence of a clean heart and peace of mind on the body. Swiss doctor Paul Tournier, in his book *A Doctor's Case Book in the Light of the Bible* (pp. 151–52), tells of a girl treated several months for anemia without success. As a last resort the doctor sent her to another doctor for a second opinion before sending her to a sanatorium. The second doctor reported that his lab work did not indicate serious anemia. The first doctor ordered another blood test which corroborated the second physician's opinion. So he asked the patient if anything out of the ordinary had taken place in her life since her previous visit. "Yes," she replied, "I've suddenly been able to forgive someone against whom I bore a nasty grudge; and at once I felt as if I could at last say yes to life!" With the lifting of her burden, the very state of her blood had changed, says Tournier.

● *The healing of his body.* When the ruthless, religious committee of investigators, who were seeking to trap Jesus, heard Him claiming to forgive sins, they thought they had Him cornered—He was guilty of blasphemy, for only God could forgive sin. Jesus' declaration of forgiveness was indeed either a case of blasphemy or God Almighty talking. Jesus did claim to be God, one of whose prerogatives He was now claiming to assume, the authority to forgive sin. Here was light shining in darkness but darkness not comprehending it.

Knowing their thoughts, Jesus asked, "Is [it] easier to say to the sick of the palsy, 'Thy sins be forgiven thee'; or to say, 'Arise, and take up thy bed, and walk'? But that ye may know that the Son of man hath power on earth to forgive sins . . . I say unto thee [addressing the palsy victim], 'Arise, and take up thy bed, and go thy way into thine house.' " Whether Jesus had the authority to forgive sin was a question that could be endlessly and indecisively debated, but whether or not He had the power to heal could be decided immediately on the spot. At Jesus' command the paralytic rose immediately, lifted the cot on which he had been carried, and walked away. He who had been a burden for years now picked up the burden of his own bed, and his restored legs now carried him away. The four friends didn't need to transport him back home. The scribes were silenced and the crowd astounded.

Now that the crippled had risen and walked as directed, who would dare question Jesus' previous claim of forgiving the man's sins. The demonstration of His power through healing was visible proof that He had the authority, which only God possessed, to forgive sin. The healing of the body was evidence He could heal the soul. The outward miracle signified that inward forgiveness had taken place. The scribes should have drawn this conclusion.

In the few moments the paralytic lay at the feet of Jesus before the physical cure, his soul had been cleansed and renewed in his Maker's image. He had been justified in God's sight. He now possessed eternal life. All else that happened that day, including the cure of body, was secondary, illustrating and augmenting what the inward regeneration had achieved. Sooner or later he would again become sick and ultimately die. But because he was forgiven, his soul would go to be with the Lord, and someday he would receive a perfect, incorruptible body.

Forgiveness is the thread that runs through all the miracle stories. When a miracle occurs, the miracle isn't the important thing. Forgiveness is the main item. When the blind were healed, it pictured the opening of the eyes to the Gospel of forgiveness. When deaf ears were unstopped, it illustrated the understanding of the heart to receive remission of sins. When the lame leaped, it portrayed a person previously unable to walk for God now walking in newness of life after removal of iniquities. Isaiah predicted the exciting miracles of Jesus: "Then the eyes of the blind shall be opened, and the ears of the deaf shall be unstopped. Then shall the lame man leap as an hart, and the tongue of the dumb sing" (35:5-6).

But Isaiah also wrote of a "new thing" God would do for His people: "I, even I, am He that blotteth out thy transgressions for Mine own sake, and will not remember thy sins" (43:25). This new thing was fulfilled by God's Son, who came to earth to suffer for the sins of mankind. His ministry, accompanied by signs and wonders, led to a cross, an empty tomb, the ascension, and to the right hand of God from which He has continued through the centuries, as He had done that day in Capernaum, to forgive sins. The self-righteous often say, "You made your bed, and so you must lie on it." But Jesus says, "Your sins are forgiven. Take up your bed and walk." The miracle of forgiveness is one that God does not want us to miss. And the forgiven person will be able to walk paths he didn't previously traverse—the highway of holiness with its bypaths of honesty, chastity, integrity, marital fidelity, love of family, clean language, respect for life, contentment, and a forgiving spirit.

Who had joy that day? The carping scribes whose hard hearts preferred an argument in theology over the healing of a sick man? The selfish crowd at the door who wouldn't let him in? The bench warmers who hadn't brought any needy person? Or these four friends? These four men were the ones who rejoiced that day. Who has joy today? Those who go out of their way to bring others to Christ. Matthew Henry wrote, "I would think it a greater happiness to gain one soul to Christ than mountains of gold and silver to myself."

We may have to keep on bringing a friend to Christ for a long time. Ted DeMoss, a former president of Christian Business Men's Committee of USA, tells of once reading John 3:1-18 to an 81-year-old man, then asking the Lord for wisdom concerning the next step. To DeMoss' surprise, as he looked over at the old man, his beard was wet with tears. DeMoss asked, "Would you like to invite Jesus Christ into your life right here?"

The man replied, "I want to do it with Mother."

Puzzled at this statement from an 81-year-old, DeMoss asked, "Where is your mother?" The man led DeMoss into the kitchen where the man's 98-year-old invalid mother sat in a canvas-backed chair. When he said, "This man has been reading the Bible to me, and I'm going to accept Jesus Christ," the woman let out a piercing scream. Regaining her composure, she said, "Mister, I don't know who you are, but I have prayed for my boy every day for over 80 years. I knew Jesus Christ as my personal Saviour when my son was born, and I've prayed for him all these years" (Ted DeMoss and Robert Tamasey, *The Gospel and the Brief Case,* CBMC Publications, Chattanooga, Tenn., 1984, pp. 36–38).

DeMoss also tells of inviting a neighbor and his wife to dinner one Friday night hoping to interest them in a four-session Bible study. Though the neighbor accepted the dinner invitation, he and his wife failed to show up. DeMoss went to his house, two doors away, to remind them of their date, but was met by the amazing reply, "We're not coming. We heard you are religious people, and we don't want to get involved with you." When DeMoss told him the food was ready, the neighbor told DeMoss to eat twice as much, firmly insisting he was not coming.

For eight years DeMoss tried to befriend his neighbor but without success. He was never able to speak directly with him, nor did the man return any of his phone calls. Suddenly one noon the neighbor showed up at the Christian Business

Men's luncheon and, finding out DeMoss was the speaker, seemed embarrassed. When DeMoss tried to speak to him after the meeting, he turned and walked away. Then DeMoss discovered he had indicated on his card that at that meeting he had prayed to accept Christ as his Saviour.

Next morning DeMoss, able to get through to his neighbor by phone for the first time in eight years, invited him to a scheduled CBMC prayer breakfast and Bible study. At the breakfast, as customary, they passed out cards with the names of men who didn't know Christ. The neighbor took two or three cards off the top and joined a small group. Looking at the cards in his hand, he noticed one of them had his name on it. He asked why. DeMoss explained that for eight years the group had prayed for him at each weekly breakfast. When it was his turn to pray, he simply said, "Dear God, thank You for these men."

CBMC has produced a helpful tool for use by those who want to bring others to Christ. It is a card titled "Ten Most Wanted Men."

Small enough to fit into a wallet or shirt pocket, it lists the names of 10 people who do not know the Lord, and the person carrying the card prays daily for every person listed till he comes to Christ. One CBMCer told DeMoss he was now on his fourth card of new names. Often a member is present at a CBMC meeting when one of his "Ten Most Wanted Men" makes a decision for Christ (DeMoss, *Ibid.*, pp. 56–59).

Do you suppose the four friends of the paralytic had a "Ten Most Wanted" list? If so, do you think he was on it?

But more importantly, do you maintain some form of a "Most Wanted" list?

DEMONS CAST OUT

I n 1986 when evangelist Jack Van Impe did a TV special on the activities of Satan and his demonic hordes, he explained how a Christian can live a victorious life free from fear and Satan's control. Aired over most major TV markets in America, the program evoked a huge response. In addition to many phone calls, about 60,000 people responded by letter. Many had prayed for victory from a life messed up by the occult, devil worship, and demon-possession. One person wrote, "I have demons in my body. I have tried everything and can't get rid of them. I pray night and day. I need your help. Send me your book on the subject."

Several times in the Gospels we meet people dominated by demons. In Jesus' day most people believed not only in the existence of demons, but that thousands waited to do them harm. These invisible powers, the people concluded, lived in unclean places like tombs, and in deserts where there was no cleansing water. Hence the expression "howling desert." Demons posed danger particularly to night travelers, newlyweds, women in childbirth, and children after nightfall. Demons were to blame for not only mental illness and epileptic seizures but for all physical diseases.

With such all-encompassing belief in demons, though a mixture of truth and superstition, Jesus devoted much of His miracle-working power to this area. In fact, more miracles have to do with the casting out of demons than with any other malady. Seven of the 35 specific instances (20 percent) of His miracles deal with victory over the demon world. In addition to these specific cases, general references to demon expulsion occur in all Synoptic Gospels (e.g., Matt. 4:24; 8:16; Mark 1:39; 3:11; Luke 10:17-20). The instructions to the Twelve in connection with their Galilean mission mentions authority over demons as a special category separate from curing illnesses (Luke 9:1). Also, the mention of Mary Magdalene among the women who financially supported Jesus' ministry adds this descriptive clause, "from whom seven demons had come out" (Luke 8:2, NIV). Here is the list of the seven specific occasions when Jesus expelled demons:

1. The demoniac in the Capernaum synagogue (Mark 1:21-28; Luke 4:31-37);
2. The man both blind and dumb (Matt. 12:22-24; Luke 11:14);
3. The two demoniacs of Gadara (Matt. 8:28-34, NIV; Mark 5:1-20; Luke 8:26-39);
4. The man with a dumb spirit (Matt. 9:32-34);
5. The Syrophenician's daughter (Matt. 15:21-28; Mark 7:24-30);
6. The boy the disciples couldn't heal (Matt. 17:14-21; Mark 9:14-29; Luke 9:37-43);
7. The woman with the spirit of infirmity (Luke 13:10-17).

We shall examine the Gadarene incident in which, according to Matthew, two demoniacs were healed. But we will follow Mark and Luke, who mention just one. This casting out was one of the most remarkable, though puzzling, of all the Gospel expulsions.

The miracle may well have taken place in the moonlight. It was evening when Jesus and His disciples entered the boat to cross Galilee (Mark 4:35). So tired that He fell asleep in a violent storm, Jesus had to be awakened in hopes He could keep the boat from capsizing. It likely was still dark when Jesus and His disciples reached shore. Perhaps the light of the moon enabled the madman to see them still a distance away. The scene was grim and eerie. The location was the area of Decapolis, a confederacy of ten cities founded after Alexander the Great's campaign, with a mixed population engaging in customs repulsive to strict Jews, such as swine-raising. Jesus, who had just stilled the storm on a lake, was about to quell the storm in a wretch's life.

Meeting the Wild Man

Beaching their boat, the disciples climbed the hill that rose from the shore. Suddenly the hush was broken by the shrill screams of a demon-possessed man leaping toward them, a fearful sight; he was dirty and his hair was matted, and in his hand he held a jagged stone with which he gashed himself, leaving streams of fresh and coagulated blood disfiguring his naked body. After his encounter with Jesus, he was found dressed.

No one would approach this madman, but his living among desolate tombs made his isolation doubly sure, for cemeteries were off-limits to Jews. The man was violent. Attempts were made to bind him, but though chained hand and foot, he tore the chains apart. His wrists, arms, and feet bore the marks of the chains. Night and day he would cut himself with stones and cry out among the tombs.

Modern travelers tell of seeing similar cases—ferocious men who wander about the mountains and sleep in tombs. They suffer paroxysms in which their prodigious strength makes them unmanageable. They run naked wildly about the countryside.

Many counselors would diagnose the man as suffering from a manic-depressive psychosis, and would consider all New Testament demon-possession as mental illness. A prescientific world, they would say, would blame physical problems with unusual manifestations on the demonic world but, with our advanced knowledge, such problems should be consigned to psychiatry.

In answer, we say that accepting the Bible as God's Word requires accepting the reality of demon-possession. The New Testament record shows clearly that Jesus Christ believed in the demon world.

Demon-Possession Today

Do demons exist and exert influence today? The Bible teaches that we struggle not against flesh and blood but "against the powers of this dark world and against the spiritual forces of evil in the heavenly realms" (Eph. 6:12, NIV). In his book *Healing and the Scriptures,* noted English preacher-physician D. Martyn Lloyd-Jones wrote that demonic activity is on the increase due to the general godlessness in society, the increased dabbling in the occult in its various forms, and the revolt against reason in favor of experience (Oliver-Nelson Books, Nashville, Tenn., 1988, pp. 158–73).

Lloyd-Jones divides the contemporary phenomena into two groups: demonic oppression and demonic possession. Dealing first with oppression, he lists four diagnostic clues relating to satanic attacks against saints today, as he observed them.

First, sudden onset of the condition. Second, unexpected behavior. Third, extreme weakness. Fourth, no response to medical treatment, baffling those who render medical or psychiatric treatment.

Turning to demonic possession, Lloyd-Jones also gives in his book four diagnostic points: a history of dabbling with spiritualism and the occult; dual personality; alternation between normal and abnormal behavior; and violent reaction to the name of Jesus and to the mention of the blood of Christ or of His coming in the flesh. Lloyd-Jones, who died prior to the publication of his book, held that it is possible for a believer to open the door to evil powers.

Missionaries on many fields relate firsthand experiences with demons. In 1986 Dr. Peter Stam, then U.S. director of the Africa Inland Mission, offered AIM supporters a booklet about an African national who spent over 25 years as a missionary to his own people. Titled *A Missionary Called Peter,* the booklet told the story of Peter Kisula, who, as a young man on his apparent deathbed in a hospital, fought a terrifying three-day battle against the demons his ancestors had worshiped for generations. Hearing the youth's torment, a nearby Christian patient urged Peter to call on Jesus who, the Christian said, was more powerful than all the demons. Peter's pulse quickened, for he had heard of this Jesus before from the lips of Africa Inland missionaries who came each week to the hospital to preach the Gospel. In the dark hospital room, the Christian prayed with Peter, who then fell into peaceful sleep. It had taken seven years for Peter to receive Christ, but then he completed Bible school, became a pastor, and later a missionary to the nomadic Turkana tribe of northern Kenya, where he established many churches, clinics, and schools.

Leadership magazine carried a forum titled "Facing the Wreckage of Evil" in which four respected leaders exchanged viewpoints on spiritual warfare. One of the four, Dr. Timothy Warner, director of professional doctoral programs at Trinity Evangelical Divinity School, declared in his final statement, "Demons are able to cause harm, and we need to be ready to deal with them, but not from a stance of fear or subservience. We don't operate toward victory; we operate out of victory. Christ won an absolute victory at the Cross" (1986, fall quarter, p. 140).

Though demon possession and mental illness are not the same, demon possession may unbalance a person and bring about mental illness. But we must be ever so careful not to find a demon in every emotional affliction. Great danger exists when an irresponsible discerner claims to know that a demon inhabits another person. It would be folly to treat mental illness as if it were demon possession. The gift of discernment is necessary to differentiate between evil spirits and mental illness. Only the qualified should undertake to minister to either the mentally ill or demon-oppressed.

At a professional seminar on satanism held in Berkeley, California in 1986 and sponsored by Spiritual Counterfeits Project and Evangelical Ministries to New Religions, cult expert James Bjornstad made the claim that out of some 500 to 600 cases he has studied, he believes only nine were legitimate cases of demon-possession. According to Bjornstad, Christian leaders are too willing to blame physical and emotional afflictions on demon-possession which he believes is limited to nonbelievers (*Eternity*, May 1986, p. 10).

Bjornstad takes a dim view of Christian exorcists who, while casting out alleged demons from believers, engage in extensive discourses with demons. Other seminar speakers seemed to agree with Bjornstad's general analysis that, while the forces of evil are certainly at work in the world, and that overt cases of dramatic, genuine demonic power occur, the one behind it all, responsible for all evil, often works out of sight.

The demon-possessed Gadarene pictures the uncontrollable nature of fallen man today, though we do not mean that the person who lives an unruly life is demon-possessed. But rather, just as the physically blind symbolize the spiritually blind and the lame those who cannot walk the paths of righteousness, so the demon-possessed typify those who live lawless, disordered lives.

A deep, underlying similarity exists between our world and the Gadarene's primitive society. People today are just as depraved, wicked, cruel, and militant. The morning newspaper and the evening TV news clearly show this with accounts of wars, terrorism, murders, outbreaks of juvenile delinquency, widespread drug addiction, mob hysteria, violence, and sexual immorality.

The civil authorities of Gadara doubtless did their best to contain this wild man and maintain public decency and order. Despite stronger and stronger chains, which worked for a short time, he broke free. Another wave of disorder soon followed. Likewise, the evil nature of man cannot be tamed by regulations, reformation, political programs, or social panaceas.

Regardless of the extent of demon-possession today, whether rare or more prevalent than we think, the influence of the devil is widespread and quite evident. The news is full of crimes—thefts, muggings, murders, kidnappings, and terrorism. We designate these heinous acts as devilish, diabolical, demonic. Just as the Gadarene was anguished by demons, so similarly people today are tortured by evil passions which dominate body and soul: lust, envy, anger, greed, drugs, alcohol.

The poor Gadarene was torn within himself, isolated from others and alienated from God. Within raged a storm that needed to be stilled just as much as the stormy Galilean waves a few hours before. Beyond human power, under Satan's control, breaking the bounds of decency, with all faculties directed to self-injury, where would he get help?

The Encounter with Jesus

When this demented man saw Jesus climbing up from the shore, he ran to meet Him. For Jesus to stand there calmly while the disordered man approached was dangerous indeed, showing His sheer courage in the presence of a man who could snap chains almost at will. The poor man must have felt some desire for wholeness, for he fell on his knees at Jesus' feet, which became a meeting place of three worlds: the underworld of evil spirits, this world of human experience, and the overworld of divine power.

Jesus commanded the demons to leave. They immediately admitted His authority, crying out, "What do You want with me, Jesus, Son of the Most High God? Have You come to torture us before the appointed time? I beg You, don't torture me!" (*The Gospels Interwoven*, Kermit Zarley, Victor, 1987, p. 111) Just as wind and wave knew Him and recognized His authority, so did these demons. Not only were they aware of who He was, but they also knew of a coming judgment, which they hoped was yet future.

Then Jesus asked his name. He answered, "Legion," which means "many." An associate editor of *Psychology Today* wrote, "Multiple-personality disorder is an affliction that fascinates and yet invites skepticism. Its symptoms are so bizarre that even some mental-health professionals doubt its existence and attribute the behavior to accomplished acting" (*Psychology Today*, February 1988, p. 80). Is not demon-possession a possible explanation in some cases?

Why did the name *Legion* come springing to his lips? Living in occupied country, the man had often seen a Roman legion with up to 6,000 soldiers clanking along the road with all its armor. Did he feel that a battalion lived inside him? Or, had some atrocity been committed against him in youth by some legionnaire.

The demons begged Jesus not to send them to the Abyss (home of the lost dead), but to permit them to enter the large herd of swine feeding on a nearby hillside. Jesus said, "Go!" When the demons came out, they entered the pigs. The herd, about 2,000 in all, stampeded down the steep bank into the lake and drowned. When exorcists in times past cast out a demon, they often placed a glass of water nearby, which was knocked over by the departing demon to prove that he had departed. This swine demonstration would now convince the Gadarene that the legion of demons had now completely left him. He could exclaim, "I'm free!"

The ultimate end of the rule of Satan over a world hostile to God was now guaranteed. Said Jesus, "But if I drive out demons by the Spirit of God, then the kingdom of God has come upon you" (Matt. 12:28, NIV). One proof of the kingdom's arrival was the rout of demons. Then through His death on the cross, Jesus "disarmed the principalities and powers and made a public example of them, triumphing over them" (Col. 2:15, RSV). The kingdom would not come in its fullness till the Second Coming, but the liberation of the Gadarene was a foretaste of a completely redeemed world still awaiting fulfillment.

Reactions Vary

● *The people.* This is one of two destructive miracles performed by Jesus, the other being the withering of the fig tree to be discussed in a later chapter. But in reality, His miracle of drowned swine had its constructive side. First, He showed His power over evil spirits. Second, He rebuked the townsfolk for violating God's law against raising unclean animals. His cleansing of the man was a blessing; His dealing with the town was a rebuke in which, though acting destructively, He was nevertheless acting righteously.

The story involves a startling paradox. When witnesses told the area folk how the widely known madman had been healed by Jesus, we would expect to hear this reaction: "They glorified God and begged Jesus to remain in their neighborhood." Instead, the record reads, "And they began to beg Him to depart from their neighborhood." In sweeping out forbidden traffic, Jesus had fingered their vested interests. They were not thinking of the demented man's welfare but of their swine. They were bothered by their financial setback. Two thousand pigs were of more value to them than one man. These people were possessed by "demon greed." It was more deeply a contest between pigs and Christ. They did not wish their life-style disturbed, so begged Him to leave their region. They should have fallen at His feet, begging deliverance from their own sins. Jesus granted their request and left.

When Paul and Silas healed a demented girl in Philippi, her masters became enraged because their way of making easy money had been removed. They took steps to see that the apostles were punished. Drug pushers care more for money than for people. On the other hand, one businessman who was brought to my attention no longer sells liquor or pornographic literature in his store, valuing persons above pigs.

● *The ex-demoniac.* The man now sat at Jesus' feet, the exact opposite of his previous condition, calm, peaceful, clothed, perhaps wearing a cloak someone had just given him. The people who came because they heard what had happened saw wonderful evidence of Christ's power to release Satan's slaves. Nothing is more striking than the conversion of a person translated out of the kingdom of darkness into the marvelous light of the Gospel. Many are the trophies of grace who have been delivered from the bondage of sin. Jesus' authority is still with us to overcome the invisible, spiritual enemy laboring night and day to destroy us.

In contrast to the area folk who wished Jesus to leave, here was one man who wanted to cling to Jesus forever. As Jesus was climbing into the boat, the ex-demoniac begged to go with Him. But Jesus refused, saying, "Go home to your family and tell them how much God has done for you, and how the Lord has had mercy on you." So the man went not only to family and friends, but to the whole broad community in which he lived, including the 10 cities known as the Decapolis, telling how much Jesus had done for him and amazing all the people. New converts sometimes prefer getting away from those who knew them at their worst, but on such our greatest impact can often be made. This man had so profoundly experienced the power of the kingdom that he could not fail as a trusted witness.

Did Jesus' command pay off? Later we find Jesus again in the Decapolis area, and this time we find Him surrounded by a great multitude, called the 4,000 whom He fed with seven loaves and a few small fishes (Mark 7:31; 8:1-9). Where did that crowd come from? Why so many in that very area where they previously begged Him to leave? Some may have been there through the testimony of this Gadarene, so wonderfully healed by Jesus.

● *Family.* What a thrill for the family when their father and husband arrived home and they realized he was at last normal. But imagine how they must have felt when they first saw him coming down the street. One of the children yells, "Father's coming!" The mother cries out, "Quick, help me barricade the door!" They move furniture against the door. Often on returning home he has beaten his wife and children and broken chairs into pieces through his demonic destructiveness. Another child says, "Why, Mother, he looks different! See his clothes! And his eyes are not wild!"

He knocks gently. "Wife, let me in. It's your husband. I don't blame you for being afraid. But I've a story to tell you. I'm a different man. I've met Jesus, and now I'm in my right mind." With much apprehension she opens the door. He takes her in his arms, calling her by endearing names of their happier years. He embraces his children one by one. "You won't need to be afraid of me anymore," he says. "You have a new husband—a new father. And we have a new home. No more demons. Jesus will run our home from now on." Through the centuries the Lord Jesus has brought peace to many a perturbed family.

Mike Godwin, on death row at the state penitentiary in Columbia, South Carolina, had the reputation as the most violent man in the prison. A jury had found him guilty of rape and murder. In his book *Twice Pardoned*, Harold Morris, himself an ex-prisoner, tells of visiting Mike Godwin. He relates, "I was told that the 21-year inmate had almost killed a guard in a fight the previous day. The warden told me the prison officials didn't know what to do with him. They led me to a dungeon-like cell with concrete walls and a metal door. The inmate walked in wearing handcuffs to keep him from hurting me. He asked me what I wanted, growling he hoped it was none of that religious junk."

Morris talked to Godwin about his violence. Godwin agreed he was the most violent man there. Morris said, "I think you're angry." To Morris' surprise Godwin agreed. Morris said he wanted to share what Jesus Christ meant to him, adding, "You see—I spent nine and a half years in prison. Six months of it was on death row, the most horrible experience of my jail life." Morris told him of the friends who gave him a Bible and Scripture verses that led him to Christ. He also told of his growth during those final five years in prison. During their hour's conversation, he also stressed the reality of Christ.

Godwin looked at Morris with tears. Saying he didn't believe in God, he asked Morris to pray for him. When Morris later spoke to the death-row inmates, Godwin, by then out of detention, came to the meeting. Afterward he asked Morris for help. Morris showed him several verses from Romans, asking him to write them down. Two days later Morris received a letter from Godwin. He told how he had gone to his death-row cell, read the verses again, and knelt to open his heart to Christ. He ended his letter, "I'd rather be here and be the man I am today than be out on the streets free. Would you help me grow?"

Morris found him a changed man, eager to learn of Christ. Like a starving man, Godwin devoured every Bible study

THE MIRACLES OF JESUS

brought him. Enrolling first in correspondence study at Columbia Bible College, he later added courses from the University of South Carolina. In 1985 he completed requirements for a two-year associate degree at the University of South Carolina, and in 1986 he received a Bachelor of Arts degree with a 3.85 grade point average. At this writing he is working on a doctorate. His death sentence has been commuted to imprisonment for life.

This once violent man, calmed by the power of Christ, has wielded a tremendous influence, not only inside prison, but outside as well through letters to young people across the country who write him about their problems.

Truly, an encounter with Jesus can make a world of difference.

SHE TOUCHED THE HEM
OF HIS GARMENT

In his book *Why Not? Accept Christ's Healing and Wholeness,* Pastor Lloyd John Ogilvie relates the experience of Jean who came forward for prayer after a morning service at the First Presbyterian Church of Hollywood. She needed courage to continue the lengthy cancer treatment and longed for healing. The answer to prayer did not result in a quick cure for the cancer but rather in a greater healing soon after.

For eight years Jean had felt "a big boulder" inside her stomach, really the weight of a resentful spirit. She had been unable to forgive her husband who divorced her after years of marriage, as well as the woman he married when the ink was scarcely dry on the divorce papers. When Jean remarried, her hurt, plus the guilt of a failed marriage, made it difficult to show love to her second husband. Then her doctor discovered a serious form of cancer. This physical and emotional stress brought her to the church to ask for prayer.

One afternoon not long later, the heavy load of resentment was lifted. Though her prayer had been for healing from cancer, the Lord answered by removing her emotional ache. Then this amazing release speeded up the healing of her cancer. Ogilvie ends the story, "Now she is healed of both the carcinoma and the dreadful emotional ache" (Revell, 1984, pp. 79–80).

One day a woman with a special need made contact with Jesus in the midst of a crushing crowd. He had just returned from the eastern side of the Sea of Galilee, where He had cast out a legion of demons from the Gadarene. Expecting Him to perform more miracles, the crowd surrounded Him almost to the point of suffocation. Though curiosity motivated most of the people, at least two approached Him because of critical needs. First, Jairus, a ruler of the synagogue, fell at Jesus' feet, imploring Him to come to his house to heal his only daughter who was at the point of death. Then as Jesus started toward Jairus' home, a longtime sick woman found healing by touching the hem of His garment. Though she attempted to keep the event a secret, Jesus stopped and forced her into the open, confirming her faith, and comforting her spirit. Really an interruption of an interruption, this parenthetical miracle is found in three Gospels (Matt. 9:20-22; Mark 5:25-34; Luke 8:43-48).

Her Sorry Situation

● *She was a woman.* What a contrast between Jairus and this woman! He was the respected leader of the synagogue; she, a social outcast. He was a man; she, a woman.

Women possessed an inferior status in the Hebrew culture of that day. Though no division of the Mishnah (the oral law) dealt solely with men, one of the six major divisions was devoted completely to rules for women. Women were excluded from public life and confined to work around the house. A woman could be divorced for talking to a man on the street. A wife was obligated to obey her husband. In life-threatening situations he must be saved first. Her most important job was to bear male babies. Childlessness was a divine curse. Women could not go beyond the Court of the Gentiles and the Women's Court in the temple area. Women were not permitted to study the Torah, or pronounce a benediction, or appear as a witness in court. Women were placed in the same category as slaves and children.

In revolutionary fashion Jesus broke this taboo. How often He treated women kindly, even numbering them among His close followers. In addition to healing this woman, He worked miracles for several others, including Peter's mother-in-law, Mary Magdalene, the woman bent over for 18 years, Jairus' daughter, and the Syrophoenician's daughter.

● *She was physically ill.* For 12 years this desperate, hurting woman had suffered a most exhausting and distressing malady, an incurable hemorrhaging. The Talmud lists at least 11 cures for this trouble, then common in Palestine. Though some astringents likely proved helpful in stanching the flow of blood, other remedies were such superstitious acts as carrying the ashes of an ostrich egg in a linen bag in summer and in a cotton rag in winter. To get rid of this debilitating sickness, she had tried every imaginable cure but without success. She was a "perpetual menstruant."

● *She was socially ostracized.* Tragically, this sickness made a woman ceremonially unclean. The Book of Leviticus ruled: "If a woman has a discharge of blood for many days, not at the time of her impurity, or if she has a discharge beyond the time of her impurity, all the days of the discharge she shall continue in uncleanness. . . . Every bed on which she lies . . . and everything on which she sits shall be unclean. . . . And whoever touches these things shall be unclean, and shall wash his clothes and bathe himself in water, and be unclean until the evening" (15:25-27, RSV).

No one could touch her, or her clothing, or anything she had polluted by her contact. She could not attend temple or synagogue. She was excluded from her family and could be legally divorced by her husband. In addition to the pain of her illness, and the loneliness of social segregation, tradition brutally suggested that a woman suffering from hemorrhaging so suffered because of personal immorality.

● *She was medically abused.* Not only was this woman sick and ostracized, but for 12 years she had been the victim of medical malpractice. She had lost both health and money. Mark puts it bluntly, "A certain woman, which had an issue of blood 12 years, and had suffered many things of many physicians, and had spent all that she had, and was nothing bettered, but rather grew worse . . . touched His garment" (5:25-27). Dr. Luke surprisingly admits, "A woman having an issue of blood 12 years, which had spent all her living upon physicians, neither could be healed of any . . . touched the border of His garment" (8:43-44). Losing self-respect and womanly dignity, she reached the point of hopeless dejection. Contrast her 12 years of misery with the 12 years of delight which Jairus' daughter had brought to her parents. Twelve years of song and sunshine in Jairus' home as opposed to 12 years of sickness, frustration, weakness, isolation, and a losing struggle of this woman to regain her health.

● *She typified a hopeless sinner.* In his book *The Miracles of Our Lord,* Dr. Charles Ryrie calls her healing "a parable of salvation." Her condition typifies all humanity: sin-sick, polluted, alienated from others and from God, and hopelessly unable to find a cure among the so-called doctors of the soul.

● *She knew she was sick.* She had a jump on many a sick person who, though up and around, doesn't realize his or her precarious physical condition. No one had to convince her that her strength was steadily declining. So she sought help from the doctors, one after another. But many persons do not realize that they possess the malady of sin and need to go to the Great Physician, like the church at Laodicea which thought itself rich and in need of nothing, but was really wretched, miserable, poor, and blind. Would you permit the Great Physician to bend over you and examine you, and would you submit to His diagnosis? Do you have a clean heart? Or is the Physician's word correct when He says that the heart is deceitful above all things and desperately wicked, and that from it proceed evil thoughts, adulteries, thefts, murders, blasphemies, and pride? The touch of sin is on every one of our members, including mind, emotions, tongue, hands, and memories. Our will is so feeble to do good! Though others could detect her paleness, no one knew of her illness better than she.

● *She consulted various doctors.* How interesting would be a complete case history of all her visits to doctors, including the treatment they prescribed. Let's picture some doctors people visit today in their hopes for a cure for their plague of sin:

● *DR. RESOLUTION.* When a patient comes to him, he advises, "Just turn over a new leaf." Invariably he gives this prescription around New Year's Day. So the patient forms a new resolution, and even writes it down, but invariably the resolution is soon broken, for we do not have strength to keep our resolve. The poor woman could not get better by just resolving, because within her was a plague which needed to be cured. Paul, speaking of a struggle within him between good and evil, ended by crying out, "O wretched man that I am! who shall deliver me from the body of this death?" His answer was, "I thank God through Jesus Christ our Lord" (Rom. 7:24-25). We cannot make ourselves better by just resolving to do better. We need the Great Physician.

● *DR. CHARACTER.* This popular physician prescribes the pursuit of a lofty ideal, like the Ten Commandments or the Sermon on the Mount. "If you keep these laws, you'll certainly be well," he promises. But no person, outside of Jesus Christ, has ever kept God's precepts perfectly. Sin cannot be cured by our own efforts of morality. We need Christ's forgiveness and the Spirit's indwelling power.

● *DR. EXAMPLE.* This doctor holds up the model of Jesus, urging us to walk in His steps. To pattern our lives after His makes us the person God wants us to be. But what good does it do for a doctor to point a physically ill man to a healthy man with the advice, "That man is well. Be like him"? The patient needs a cure that will get to the root of his trouble, which is his sinful heart.

● DR. MIND-OVER-MATTER. This doctor says, "If you think correctly, you'll be all right." He has all kinds of medicines, such as Christian Science, New Thought, Positive Thinking. He claims that through right thinking the mind can bring utopia. But the mind is also contaminated by the plague of sin and needs the touch of the Great Physician.

● DR. CHURCHMAN. According to this physician, healing comes through some ecclesiastical ceremony. So he sends people to various churches, saying that if they get christened, baptized, say their prayers, attend services, take communion, or join the church, they'll go to heaven. But these external cures have as much value as applying rubbing alcohol on the chest when cancer is eating away at some vital internal organ.

After years of going the rounds of doctors, the poor woman had lost all her money, which may have been a blessing, because with any money left, she might have tried still another doctor. Now with neither health nor money, where could she go? She decided to throw herself on the mercy of Jesus. It's when we are poor in spirit, at our wits' end, and knowing that we cannot cure ourselves that we are ready for the help of Dr. Jesus. The hymn-writer put it, "Just as I am, poor, wretched, blind . . . O Lamb of God, I come! I come!"

Her Desperate Faith

At the lowest ebb of depression, after 12 years of wasting illness, this confirmed invalid found a glimmer of hope. Her faith was fueled by reports of others healed—a man delivered of an unclean spirit, Peter's mother-in-law healed of a fever, a leper cleansed—all by a man called Jesus. The leprosy incident interested her greatly because, like her, he was untouchable; yet the Master had broken the rule against touching a leper and had healed him. Jesus even healed on the Sabbath. A current of hope surged within her. She had to see Him. Perhaps she thought, *If I can get near enough to Him, some flow of power from Him will cure my illness.*

She was among that crowd awaiting His return from across the lake, pressing with expectancy past the edge of the crowd. Perhaps she saw Him step out of the boat. As she saw His compassionate face, confidence surged within. Some think her inner transformation from fearful anguish to faithful anticipation a greater wonder than the miracle itself. Freed from her doubts, she then determined somehow to make contact with Jesus. Perhaps He could meet her overwhelming needs. Her faith was stirred to still greater heights when she saw Jesus respond to Jairus' plea by heading toward his house.

This pitiful woman would never have come to Jesus had not others told her of His wonder-working power. Without radio, TV, or newspapers, the wonder of His healing power, passed by word of mouth alone, drew thousands to hear Him in person. How much more with today's avenues of communication should our witness help others come to faith in the Saviour's availability and power.

● *Her mixed faith.* How could she make contact with Jesus? She would be too ashamed to go to Him directly and speak of her sickness. She couldn't ask Him to lay His hands on her because she was an untouchable. In fact, everyone she brushed against in the crowd became ceremonially unclean from that contact. As she succeeded in getting closer to Jesus, she wondered what to do. Suddenly she decided. If He touched her, He might be considered unclean. But if she touched Him, *That would do it,* she thought. *Perhaps a cure can be made by the bare touch of anything connected with Him, even without Him knowing it, and though it be but the tassel on His cloak.*

In those days devout Jews wore tassels at the corners of their outer garments, as dictated in the Law: "The Lord spake unto Moses, saying, 'Speak unto the Children of Israel, and bid them that they make them fringes in the borders of their garments throughout their generations' " (Num. 15:37-38). The purpose was to remind them, as they put on their clothes

97

in the morning or took them off at night or wore them during the day, to obey all God's commands. Jesus obeyed this precept. Concentrating on one of His tassels, the woman thought, *That's what I'll touch.*

Her faith was mingled with superstition. In his book *Mark: The Servant Gospel,* Dr. Donald Grey Barnhouse comments:

> She thought that there was some magical power going forth from Jesus' physical body rather than power going forth from His omnipotent and sovereign will. It was a faith that was supremely ignorant. It was the same kind of faith encouraged by certain healers of today, who say, "Put your hand on the radio and send me a dollar," or, "Buy the special charm." She had no concept of the fact that true life comes from Christ's sovereign grace and that His compassion goes out to save, heal, and bless by an act of His will. She thought that it would be possible to sneak a blessing and slip away without being caught. There is no knowledge of Christ's identity and His ways of working. . . . Yet her heart was hungry to be whole and to be freed from her misery. She was confident that just a touch would somehow be enough. And, though so imperfect, this was enough to receive the grace of Christ! In light of this, we must not condemn a person who does not subscribe to every point of our creed. True faith may be based on a very hazy mental perception of partial truth. In Latin America, the illiterate Indian who burns candles before a shrine may have the light of Christ. The hand that holds a crucifix may yet touch the cross. The face of Christ may be visible through a cloud of incense. Every day, more and more, I thank God that I have nothing to do with deciding who is saved and who is not (Victor Books, 1988, pp. 55–56).

Her faith, though feeble, flawed, superstitious, and selfish, was nevertheless exercised and effective.

● *Her personal touch.* Perhaps her outcast status helped

as the crowd, recognizing an untouchable, quickly moved aside to avoid any contact. In her weakness she stumbled closer and closer, muttering, "All I need is a touch." Then lunging forward, she knelt behind Christ and touched the tassel. Instantaneously, a hot flash pulsated through her. The bleeding stopped. Mark says, "Straightway the fountain of her blood was dried up; and she felt in her body that she was healed of that plague" (5:29). She knew she was cured.

You ask, "How may I touch Christ now?" The very act of talking with Him is touching Him. If you know the plague of your heart, if you have come to see that none but Jesus can meet the need of helpless sinners, and if your heart cries out to Him, then you are touching Him. His righteousness will be imputed to you; your sins will be washed away; and His resurrection life will be communicated to you by the power of the Spirit. The Bible reminds us how close God is: "For the word is nigh thee, even in thy mouth, and in thy heart" (Rom. 10:8). We don't have to climb up to heaven to bring Christ down, or descend into the depth to bring Him up, but as the next verse promises, "That if thou shalt confess with thy mouth the Lord Jesus, and shalt believe in thine heart that God hath raised Him from the dead, thou shalt be saved" (v. 9). Significantly, Jesus would then lead her into open confession, for He well knew that "with the heart man believeth unto righteousness; and with the mouth confession is made unto salvation" (v. 10).

How little it takes to get saved. The Bible speaks of believing, repenting, coming, looking, hearing, tasting, turning, or trusting. No need to beg, cajole, cry, or coax. Jesus didn't send her a bill. She could pay nothing, for she was bankrupt. The heart that reaches out in genuine repentance and faith toward Christ has His cleansing. This miracle encourages the same simple, straightforward approach to Jesus today.

Her Public Confession

Though certainly the tassel of His garment could have been touched without His knowledge, Jesus became aware that someone was touching Him, not with accidental contact, but with nervous finger and conscious effort. Quickly He understood its meaning—another needy soul victimized by this world's woes was drawing near for mercy. Willingly, He released His power to heal her. So He asked, "Who touched Me?" When Peter replied that many people were pressing against Him, Jesus insisted, "Someone touched Me; I know that power has gone out from Me" (Luke 8:45-46, NIV). Every time Jesus healed, it cost Him something.

- *Thronging or touching Jesus?* Crowds were jostling Jesus but only one person made vital contact. What a huge difference between her and the masses! The desperate woman alone in her plight received His cleansing. Doubtless many had physical problems which could have been met by His power had they the faith of this woman. But though they pushed and shoved around Jesus, no others were healed. Augustine put it, "Many thronged Him, but one touched Him."

People still throng Him today in evangelistic crusades, Easter services, rescue missions and Worldwide Communion Sunday gatherings. Many who attend have their names on church rolls, yet in the thick of the multitude they have never reached out a hand to make life-changing contact with the Lord Himself. Until we acknowledge, "Lord, I am a sinner; I suffer the plague of iniquity; I've come to the end of my rope; I thank You for dying as my Saviour; I now turn in repentance from wrong and commit my soul to You," we have not exercised faith personally, and are still thronging but not yet touching.

The woman became the focal point of the Saviour's attention. He could immediately sift out the desire for mercy midst the noisy babble of the crowd. He could have brushed her off by saying that He was on an emergency mission to Jairus' home. But He took time to show kindness to an insignificant woman. Not lost in the crowd, she became the one individual who mattered the most at the moment. Does the inclusion of long genealogies in the Bible indicate that in God's sight man is neither a mere species, nor an unimportant creature, nor an abstraction, nor a subordinate to the state, but a person? Augustine said, "God loves each one of us as if there were only one of us to love."

● *Bringing her into the open.* Had the woman had her way, this event would never have found a place in the Gospel record. She had obtained the desired blessing and wanted to slink away unnoticed. But she would then be returning home with the mistaken notion that the power that cured her resided in the tassel, not in Christ. So Christ wanted to help her understand the true nature of faith. He called out, "Who touched Me?" As He looked in her direction, she knew she had to reveal her identity. She also knew that to do so would mean advertising her shameful illness and admitting her wrong in joining a crowd and touching Jesus. Moved by gratitude because of her instantaneous healing, yet trembling, she confessed "all the truth" (Mark 5:33), including her debilitating malady, the 12 years of suffering, the isolation, the hopeless outlook. The typical religious leader would have cursed the polluted woman and hurried away for ceremonial cleansing. But she found Jesus kind and supportive.

The Lord's work was not finished as long as she remained a secret follower. He wants no "closet" disciples. How wonderful when Nicodemus and Joseph of Arimathea came into the open to ask for the body of Jesus in order to give it decent burial. Jesus promised that "whosoever . . . shall confess Me before men, him will I confess before My Father which is in heaven" (Matt. 10:32). Many churches require a confession of faith before voting prospects into membership. Likewise, Jesus wanted her to give a testimony.

● *Her faith was confirmed.* At the start, the woman did not fully comprehend what she was doing. She knew little about the Messiah of Israel, nor had she likely ever been close to Him. Her doctrine consisted of one superstitious article which, according to the Greek tense, she kept repeating within: "If I may but touch His garment, I shall be whole." She needed a little more instruction, so Jesus said, "Daughter, thy faith hath made thee whole." Not magic but *faith*. Perhaps her example inspired others later to adopt the same method—touching the hem of Jesus' garment—for healing (Matt. 14:36; Mark 6:56).

Not only did He confirm her faith, but He assured her of a

bright future. He told her, "Go in peace." She was freed from her unpleasant condition. No more would it make her life miserable. This is the only time Jesus addressed a woman as "Daughter." Though both may have been about the same age, He spoke to her as a father would to his child. Or did He speak from the standpoint of the Heavenly Father's authority?

Faith does not grow in a vacuum. Faith germinates and grows by exposure to the grace and knowledge of Jesus Christ. D.L. Moody once said that for years he sought faith in the wrong place: "I prayed for faith as though someday faith would come down and strike me like lightning. But faith did not seem to come. One day I read the tenth chapter of Romans, 'Faith cometh by hearing, and hearing by the Word of God.' I had up to this time closed my Bible and prayed for faith. I now opened my Bible and began to study, and faith has been growing ever since."

Think how this event encouraged the faith of Jairus. Even as Jesus was speaking to the woman, the shocking news came that his daughter had died. Would his faith be sufficient? The woman's testimony would help overcome the doubts flooding his mind. This interruption of Jesus on the way to Jairus' home could only serve to strengthen his faith. Delays are not always denials. In fact, in God's timetable slow may be fast.

Tradition says this woman, at her own cost, erected two brass statues on a pedestal in her native city of Caesarea to commemorate her healing. These statues remained till Julian, a Roman emperor who tried to bring back the pagan gods, destroyed them and erected his own statue in place of hers, only to see his likeness blasted by a lightning bolt. One statue of hers represented a woman on her knees, with hands held out before her in the attitude of a suppliant. The other pictured a man with a cloak over his shoulder, his hand extended toward the woman.

Whenever a person in need comes begging for mercy at the feet of Jesus, the willing Saviour stands ready to bestow His forgiving grace.

A LAD
AND HIS LUNCH

At the annual convention of the National Association of Evangelicals in 1986, missionary statesman David Howard related an unforgettable experience. Traveling with a World Relief representative in Thailand and reaching the border, he learned that a quarter of a million refugees lived immediately on the other side, in a tiny strip of land boxed in by the neighboring country's army and denied admittance to Thailand.

Walking across the border and into the refugee camp, Howard sensed the overwhelming helplessness of the people. Big banners carried their pathos: "Isn't seven years of suffering enough?" and "Someone—somewhere—please help!"

A young woman of about 30 approached with five little children, Howard related, " . . . with the two saddest eyes I've ever seen in my life. She pled, "Sir, can you get me out of here? I walked for six weeks with my five children. My husband's dead. I need to get out."

● *Statistics staggering.* Today, more than 11 million peo-

ple are strangers in foreign lands, pushed out of their home-
lands by wars, government takeovers, and cultural genocides.
Another 13 million are homeless in their own countries, victims of civil wars and threats of execution, more than half of
whom are women and children.

Natural disasters, like earthquakes, volcanoes, floods, and
typhoons, kill more than 145,000 annually, leaving millions
homeless. Every day 35,000 people die of starvation, 24 every
minute, 18 of whom are children.

One day Jesus and His disciples faced what seemed an impossible situation. Five thousand men plus countless women
and children needed food. To meet this need Jesus performed
a great miracle, called the Feeding of the 5,000. Its impor-
tance is shown by its inclusion in all the Gospels, the only
miracle found in all four (Matt. 14:13-21; Mark 6:30-44; Luke
9:10-17; John 6:1-14). John selected this as one of eight miracles in his Gospel, designed to lead his readers to believe on
Jesus Christ. Performed before so many witnesses, this miracle is the best attested of His wonders. Unlike healings which
mended something, this miracle was an extension of creation,
multiplying loaves and fish to satisfy the hunger of this vast
crowd.

Overwhelming Problem

To get rest from the crowds following them and relief from the
shock of the murder of John the Baptist, Jesus and His disciples withdrew by boat across the Sea of Galilee from Capernaum to Bethsaida, about 10 miles away. Because the lake was
small, it wasn't difficult for people to follow by shore and soon
catch up. Today a church stands on the traditional site of the
miracle, called The Church of the Multiplication of the Loaves
and Fishes. On the wall is the picture of a loaf and two fishes.
The area then had about 14 cities, each with 15,000 people.

In those days people did not work from 9 to 5. Many were
bosses or part owners of small businesses, perhaps engaged in
farming or fishing. Nothing prevented them from dropping
their tasks and following this miracle worker, some in their
own small boats but most walking. One little boy after Sunday

School described them as "the multitude that loafs and fishes."

Jesus was at the peak of His popularity. By the thousands they came. Idle curiosity and love of excitement will always draw a crowd. Three verbs in John 6:2 are in the imperfect tense, indicating continuous action. It reads literally, "A great multitude *was following* Him because they *were seeing* His miracles which He *was doing*." Most deemed Him a clever magician but not the promised Messiah. Anyone who can provide food for the body will carry the vote, but when Jesus later challenged them on spiritual matters, many went back and walked no more with Him (6:66). But now people were tired, hungry, and far from home and store. How could these thousands ever be fed? How would Jesus and the Twelve react to this overwhelming problem?

Reaction of Jesus

Though Jesus knew the ulterior motive of those pursuing Him, He took compassion on them. He could have blamed them for lack of foresight in failing to bring some lunch along. But He realized they had gone a whole day without food. In addition, He saw them with spiritual need, as sheep without a shepherd.

Though Jesus cared for spiritual problems, He also had concern for physical needs. He was affected by the crowd's weariness and hunger. The Christian who alleviates human suffering does the Heavenly Father's will. Doctors, nurses, medics, helpers in soup kitchens, and relief workers who dispense food in famine areas reflect the common grace of God.

In the beginning days of The Salvation Army in London, General Booth gave people hot meals. When critics claimed that the Christian's duty was to win souls, not to care for the mere mortal body, Booth answered, "How can you warm a man's heart with the love of Christ when his feet are perishing with cold?"

Reaction of the Disciples

As the day wore on, the disciples said to Jesus, "This is a desert place, and now the time is far passed. Send them away, that they may go into the country round about, and into the

105

villages, and buy themselves bread; for they have nothing to eat" (Mark 6:35-36). When Jesus suggested feeding the crowd, the disciples regarded the situation as hopeless, especially Philip.

● *Philip.* Jesus asked Philip where they could buy bread to feed the crowd. He wasn't really asking if there were any fast-food places, diners, cafeterias, or supermarkets in the area, but He was testing Philip. Had the Twelve learned of His great power from previous miracles? Typical of the others, Philip saw only the complete hopelessness of the situation. Pressing a few buttons on his mental calculator, he figured that, even if shops were accessible, it would take more than half a year's wages to buy enough to give everyone in this multitude a bite each. His modern counterparts sit on church boards blocking every new project with, "It can't be done."

Philip calculated without faith. Depending solely on visible evidence, logic, and bottom lines, he forgot how divine power could feed the multitude. To him it was a matter of dollars and cents. His temperament tended more toward arithmetic than toward adventure. Hopefully, when day was done, he had learned to include God in his calculations. Perhaps he lamented, "I should have known. He who can still the storm, heal the sick, and change water into wine can easily feed this multitude." He learned that little is much if God is in it.

● *Andrew.* A shoe salesman, arriving in an area where everyone went barefooted, phoned his head office, "Can't sell shoes here. People don't wear them." A salesman from a competitor telegraphed his office, "Great prospects! Everybody needs shoes!" Though Philip looked at the problem negatively, Andrew took a cautiously positive attitude. He spoke up, "There is a lad here who has five barley loaves and two small fishes." Then to protect himself, he added, "But what are they among so many?" If it didn't work out, he could say, "I told you so." It was good that the boy had not come to Judas with his lunch, for Judas, probably already unhappy with the prospect of shelling out from the Twelve's meager treasury, might have followed his thieving proclivity and devoured the lunch all by himself.

But with mustard-seed faith, Andrew thought, *If the boy would give his lunch to the Master, small as it is, perhaps He would do the rest, and somehow satisfy the appetites of the crowd.* He saw the potential when he offered, "There is a lad here." Philip produced figures to show what could not be done, but Andrew, hoping something might be done, brought a boy.

A dejected freshman sat across from Dr. V.R. Edman, then president of Wheaton College in Illinois. Speechless, he pushed a slip of blue paper across the desk. It was a statement from the business office that the student's next payment was due. The student had not come to ask for financial assistance but was bewildered as to what to do next. He worked long hours to meet expenses. Despite his best efforts he did not have the resources to meet his obligation.

Noting that the bill totaled $29.75, Dr. Edman asked the young man how much he had toward the debt. Speaking for the first time, he said, "Only 75 cents." The situation seemed so impossible he thought of dropping out of school. Pushing the bill back to him, Dr. Edman said, "Just turn the statement over and write down this equation on the other side." He dictated, "Seventy-five cents are to $29.75 as. . . ." Faithfully the student began writing the equation with no idea how it would end. "Seventy-five cents are to $29.75 as 5 loaves and 2 fishes are to 5,000 men + women + children." By the time Dr. Edman reached the part about women and children, the student had stopped writing. He dropped the pencil on the desk and bowed his head to pray. Tearfully, he told the Lord that his part of the equation was far less difficult than the part about loaves and fish, and he asked forgiveness for his little faith. Dr. Edman reminded him that our part is to trust and obey.

Next day the student came excitedly to the office to tell Dr. Edman that God had wonderfully answered prayer by sending enough unexpected money to pay the bill.

After army service the freshman returned to complete college. Later when he would meet Dr. Edman at some alumni gathering, he would begin to repeat, "Seventy-five cents are to $29.75 as 5 loaves and 2 fishes are to 5,000 men + women + children."

• *The lad.* What the lad had was not much. The loaves were not like our full loaves of bread but rather like little pancakes; and the fish, like sardines. But God can take small things to do big exploits. God used a baby's tears to move Pharaoh's daughter to save Baby Moses. God used the rod of Moses to work miracles before Pharaoh. God used a sling and a stone hurled by the boy David to kill a giant. God used a little maid to bring a mighty but leprous general to Elisha for healing. Jesus took a little child to teach His disciples humility. Five loaves and two small fish, placed in the hand of Christ by an unnamed lad, became much.

The film *Twice Pardoned* traces the fall of Harold Morris from all-star athlete to death-row inmate. Shot on several locations, including Georgia State Penitentiary, the movie also tells of his transformation by Christ and dramatic pardon from a life sentence. Playing on a prison ball team, Morris one day noticed a boy sitting on a bench watching the game. Morris started toward him but a guard stopped him. Next game the guard let Morris sit on a bench and talk to the boy. The lad was wearing a T-shirt that said, "Jesus First!" He told Morris that his name was Cliff, that he was 12, that his father was a state trooper, that his mother worked as a nurse at the prison, and that he lived in a house beside the prison. Morris said, "You know I'm a convict, don't you?" The lad responded, "But I'm not afraid of you."

Cliff attended all the prison games that season, and he and Morris became close friends. After the season Cliff came to the prison fence almost every day to talk through the wire. He asked Morris many questions about life in prison and always wore a T-shirt with a Christian slogan, such as "I'm OK. Jesus don't sponsor no losers!" Morris laughed at his shirts but not at the seriousness with which he shared his faith. That boy often told Morris that he needed Jesus in his life. Cliff usually had a basketball in his hands, for he aimed to be a great basketball player. A former all-state basketball player, Morris gave him pointers to improve his game. They developed a strong friendship despite the wire barrier. While Morris instructed him about sports, the lad taught Morris about Jesus.

Morris became a Christian. One day soon after, Cliff spotted Morris with a Bible in his hand. "What are you doing with that?" he asked. Morris explained, "I've become a Christian, and I'm going to Bible study." The boy grinned, then suggested they share some Scripture. He knew 10 times as many verses as did Morris. The lad's friendship helped make Morris' bleak days bearable, and both were sad when Cliff's family moved away. Cliff handed Morris a farewell gift through the fence. It was a wooden cross made of two small shellacked branches, topped by a string so it could be hung in Morris' cell.

After not hearing from Cliff for some time, Morris learned from the lad's mother that his high school basketball team was playing in the state finals that night and it would be broadcast; Cliff wanted Morris to listen. Cliff scored 27 points, was voted the most valuable player, and was interviewed after the game. The sports announcer asked if he had been nervous. Cliff answered, "No, sir. Win or lose, I knew God was with me. You see, I'm a Christian, and everything I do in life, I do for Jesus Christ. I give Him the glory." As he listened in his cell, Morris realized he himself needed to dedicate his life fully.

Soon the warden gave Morris permission to speak in area high schools. When Cliff heard this, he insisted that Morris come to his school. Cliff introduced Morris to the student body as his friend and talked of the impact Morris had had on his life. He urged them to listen to what he had to say. At the conclusion of his talk, students gave Morris a standing ovation. Morris knew only too well that a lad had been used of God to touch his life. Nothing is small when placed in the hands of Jesus.

● *The lad with the lunch was obedient.* Somehow the lad learned of the need to feed the crowd. Perhaps it was his friendship with Andrew, or did he overhear the dialogue be-

THE MIRACLES OF JESUS

tween Jesus and Philip? When he realized that he had the only food, minimal though it was, he faced several choices. He could keep the lunch completely for himself. Had he selfishly polished it off himself, only one person's hunger would have been satisfied. Had he sold it, or traded it for some trinket, still only one person's appetite would have been met. Had he pretended he had no food and hidden it somehow, no one would have eaten it on that occasion. Had he decided to share it with only one pal, thousands would have gone hungry.

He could have said, "That's their problem. Don't expect me to feed this huge crowd!" But without anyone snatching it from his hand, he obediently gave it to Jesus with the result that thousands were fed and 12 basketfuls left over.

Over 30 years ago five young missionaries were martyred by the Auca Indians in the Ecuadorian jungle. *Life* magazine sent a reporter to cover the story. The night before his return, the writer sat with the five widows. "I leave tomorrow. I have all the facts. You've been so gracious in letting me read your husbands' letters and diaries. I've all the photos I need. You've answered my questions. But I lack one thing. I can't comprehend what made those men come here in the first place. They knew the Aucas were savage killers."

"We can answer with one word—obedience," came the explanation. "Our husbands were obedient to the last command of Jesus to go into all the world and preach the Gospel to every creature—and the Aucas are part of the world."

● *The lad saw Jesus perform a marvelous miracle.* Skeptics try to explain away the miracle this way: Though many had brought no food because of their sudden decision to follow the crowd, others did carry some provisions, intending to keep them all for themselves. But when Jesus had them sit down and then produced the five little rolls and two little fish, those who had lunches also produced their food and shared it with those who had none. Their pooled lunches provided more than enough. But this theory fails to explain why afterward the people wanted to make Jesus king. He had performed a mighty miracle, and they knew it!

● *The command to sit.* The Lord told the crowd to sit in 50s and 100s. Against the green grass, they looked like flowerbeds in a garden. The Lord does things decently and in order. Their sitting down would indicate their obedience as well as their incipient expectation of faith.

● *Giving thanks.* Saying grace for meals seems to be a fading practice. How long since you saw anyone bow his head to offer thanks before eating? Jesus blessed the food in front of thousands. To fail to thank God daily for bread is base ingratitude. I vividly recall how once, after three of us had just said grace at a restaurant in Buffalo, our waitress hurried over to ask if we were feeling all right.

● *The multiplication.* After giving thanks Jesus broke the loaves, then gave to the disciples to distribute bread to the seated groups. He also divided the fish so that everyone ate until satisfied.

The record is not clear as to where the miracle took place; was it in the hands of Jesus or in the hands of the disciples? More likely in the hands of Jesus, where new bread and new fish kept forming. Likely, each disciple had a basket which he filled, then distributed, returning for refills. The process went on uninterrupted till all were fed, showing the sufficiency of Jesus midst the deficiency of the crowds.

Note that the disciples were a link between Jesus and the hungry. Jesus works through people to reach other people. But before the disciples gave, they had to receive. Before we share spiritual food, we have to receive divine nourishment. Note that the disciples didn't keep giving to the first rows over and over but gave to everybody. We should give the Bread of Life to all nations, not just to our own communities.

When serving as a missionary in South America, David Howard traveled to a remote village for a Bible conference. Fifty were expected but 150 came. Food supplies began running out after a few days. So several men went fishing one afternoon but caught nothing. So they decided to wash their nets before going back, but prayed, "Lord, we didn't come here to fish for fun. We need food." One man capriciously cast out his net to wash it, then yelled, "Get over here, I've got a big fish!" It was a giant catfish. In the next few minutes, they caught four more large fish, providing more than enough food for the remainder of the conference.

● *A large surplus.* Not only were the crowds filled, but the disciples gathered up 12 baskets of fragments—not little scraps and crumbs but broken pieces of food still suitable for eating. Note the combination of extravagance and frugality. Though food was produced in abundance, nothing was to be lost. Each loaf was multiplied to feed a thousand men, as well as women and children; the fish, two and a half thousand. The expression of Jesus' generosity, "when they were filled," contrasts starkly with Philip's stingy "that every one of them may take a little." The disciples discovered that Jesus could do exceedingly above all that they could ask or think. Each disciple had a basketful of food which would serve him for several days. The memory of that miracle should have lingered long, yet we find that soon the disciples, confronted with a similar seemingly impossible situation, involving only 4,000 people, had forgotten this demonstration of divine power.

But the multitude was so impressed that they wanted to make Jesus king. Their substandard faith rested in a miracle worker who could relieve physical and social distress, but not in Him as the Saviour and Master of men. Still today, the candidate who can feed the populace will win the election. The prospect of perpetual free meals is almost irresistible.

A woman shared with my wife her "miracle." Along in years, the woman used her car to drive elderly people to and from church, plus other volunteer work. The car wore out, and the woman's health began to fail. Then one day came a letter. An undelivered inheritance reaching back 20 years had been collecting interest. The woman was able to buy a new car, completely paid for with a balance still in her account. Also, it happened just when the doctor said she could drive again. The woman described her experience: "It was like the leftover abundance from the loaves and fishes!"

What a story the lad had to tell when he went home. We may have the same joy if we bring our "fives and twos" to the Lord. Someone suggested each of us is made up of "fives and twos." Five fingers, two eyes. Five toes, two ears. Also two arms, two lips, two legs. The multitude is hungry. Shall we send them away or be a blessing as was the boy?

The Bread of Life

Though some general similarities exist between the feedings of the 5,000 and of the 4,000, distinct differences show them to be separate miracles, such as the numbers fed (which differ by a thousand), the basketfuls of fragments remaining (which differ by five), and the locations (which differ by miles). However, the overall lesson of both events is identical. The physical bread eaten by the multitudes would not satisfy, for they would be hungry within a few hours, again by next morning, and again and again the rest of their lives. The miraculous feeding was a short-term solution.

But this multiplication of bread became a symbolic announcement that Christ was indeed the new Bread. In the miracle He disclosed His messianic identity and paved the way for an extended discourse in which He declared, "I am the bread of life." The miracle would have conjured memories of the provision of manna during the wilderness wandering. But miraculous manna falling in the wilderness did not satisfy their fathers. Rather said Jesus, "Your fathers did eat manna in the wilderness, and are dead. This is the bread which cometh down from heaven, that a man may eat thereof, and not die. I am the living bread which came down from heaven; if any man eat of this bread, he shall live forever" (John 6:49-51).

In his book *Addresses on the Gospel of John,* Dr. Harry Ironside said, "When we recognize that His precious blood poured out on the cross has atoned for our sins, then we are eating His flesh and drinking His blood" (Loizeaux Brothers, p. 264). Believing in Christ means entering into the spiritual realities symbolized by His flesh and blood. He thus becomes our sustenance. That Christ is the Living Bread is doubtless the major lesson of this miracle.

113

THE MIRACLES OF JESUS

People everywhere, even those materially prosperous, are spiritually hungry. Pascal, the French physicist of three centuries ago, spoke of "a God-shaped vacuum in the heart of each man which cannot be satisfied by any created things, but only by God the Creator, made known through Jesus Christ," the Bread of Life. When we bring the Gospel to those who have never received the living Bread, and they receive His spiritual nourishment, we are fulfilling the promise of Jesus, "Greater works than these shall ye do."

Are you a Sunday School teacher, a youth worker, choir member? This miracle should be an encouragement to every Christian worker to present talents, gifts, and service to Him. He can multiply and bless your offering to bring lasting nourishment to those who are spiritually famished.

In a display case at Camp of the Woods in upper New York State is an American $1 bill and the story behind it. Years ago missionary John Bechtel of Hong Kong tried to raise funds for a camp ministry in his outreach to Chinese children. His only response was a $1 gift from a little girl who wanted her ice cream allowance to be used in the Lord's work.

When Christian Children's Fund decided to give up its orphanage ministry in Hong Kong, it offered Bechtel one of its properties for $250,000. With only a $1 balance, he had to decline. A year later the same organization informed Bechtel that he could have the property for a simple $1 legal purchase with the promise that the property would be used solely for presenting the Gospel of salvation to all who came within its gates. Since then, thousands of Chinese have heard the Gospel and accepted Christ at what is known as Suen Douh Camp. The ice cream allowance of a little lass, surrendered to the Lord like the loaves and fishes, has been multiplied thousands of times over in a ministry which continues to this day.

What do you have to give that the Lord might multiply?

STILLING
THE STORM

A few minutes before midnight on January 4, 1988, Operation Mobilization's missionary ship *Logos* ran aground after leaving Ushuaia, Argentina, the southernmost city of the world, while passing through the Beagle Channel toward the open seas of the South Atlantic. The jolt, accompanied by a harsh, scraping noise, sent the missionary volunteers and their families scurrying from their beds, and various items went flying in all directions. Moments later came the order, "Don't panic! Put on your life jackets!" The 141 men, women, and children, well prepared by weekly safety drills, donned warm clothes and life jackets, and reported to the dining-room area. At first, the captain hoped the rising tide would release the ship. However, with the vessel at a 20-degree list, the order was given at 5:10 A.M. to abandon ship. No one was injured in the evacuation. At 5:30 A.M. the Chilean navy rescued the crew and staff from the *Logos* lifeboats.

In its 17 years of ministry, the *Logos* had visited 402 ports in 107 countries. Over 7 million people had climbed its gangways to visit its large book exhibits. Thirty million pieces of Gospel literature had been distributed from the ship, resulting in thousands coming to Christ. Immediately a drive was launched to replace the *Logos*.

The *Logos* was not the first vessel to ferry God's servants on teaching and evangelistic missions. Jesus and the Twelve used a boat to get from place to place around the Sea of Galilee. Recently an ancient craft, described by the Israeli press as "the Jesus boat," was unearthed on the shores of Galilee. This well-preserved boat, discovered by two brothers from a nearby kibbutz, was dug up by volunteers out of the muck in which it had been buried for 2,000 years. Nobody, of course, knows for sure whether the boat existed when Christ began His ministry, much less if He ever traveled in it. Plans called for refloating the 25-foot boat, moving it a few hundred yards along the beach, and submerging it in chemical preservatives till ready for display.

Sailors on the Sea of Galilee have always faced the danger of sudden storms. The lake, 6 miles wide and 12 to 14 miles long, is 600 feet below sea level in a bowl-shaped depression, surrounded by precipitous hills. Sometimes, when the sun sets in early evening, winds rise over the Mediterranean and blow cold air inland. Reaching the Sea of Galilee, the cold air merges with warm air rising from the water, churning the lake into a foaming rage. The winds keep funneling down through the encircling hills, fueling the boiling cauldron with waves sometimes as high as six feet. Twice the Gospels tell us that Jesus stilled such a storm. The first time Jesus was asleep in the boat (Matt. 8:23-27; Mark 4:35-41; Luke 8:22-25). On the second occasion, which we will now examine, Jesus was not aboard ship with His disciples (Matt. 14:22-36; Mark 6:45-56; John 6:15-24).

The Disciples Battle a Storm
One evening the disciples had rowed their open craft a short distance out on the Sea of Galilee when they found themselves in a storm. Likely Peter took command, holding the rudder with stalwart arm, issuing orders. Calm had given way to

confusion. The tempest tossed the vessel like cork. So for all of us who sail the sea of life, occasions rise when serenity gives way to storm. Our once-smooth course is beset by wind and rain. Daylight surrenders to darkness.

Some storms are caused by Satan, like "the great wind from the wilderness" which struck the house where Job's children were dining, killing all ten of them. Other storms come through the stubbornness of others, like Paul's shipwreck in the Mediterranean which could have been avoided had those in charge not impatiently sailed despite adverse conditions. We experience some storms because of our own foolishness, like Jonah whose running away from God resulted in his being caught in a tempest that struck the ship he had boarded. The *AARP* (American Association of Retired People) *News Bulletin* (April 1988, p. 3) stated: "It is no secret that a great deal of the illness in this country is a result of personal behavior. The American Medical Association has estimated that more than half of all disease is lifestyle-related. Each year, 36 million workdays are lost because of alcohol and drug abuse, while more than 30 million workdays—and $2 billion in wages—are lost due to illnesses caused by high blood pressure." The prodigal son's own waywardness landed him in a pigpen.

● *This storm was not of the disciples' making.* The disciples found themselves in a storm because of the explicit order of their Master. Right after Jesus miraculously fed the 5,000, the multitude wanted to make Him king by force. Realizing that His popularity stemmed from His ability to provide food, and not from any spiritual reason, He sought solitude. But first He compelled "His disciples . . . to get into a ship, and . . . to go before Him unto the other side, while He sent the multitudes away. And when He had sent the multitudes away, He went up into a mountain apart to pray; and when the evening was come, He was there alone" (Matt. 14:22-23).

Jesus had to virtually force them into the boat, perhaps because they wished to be with Him if the crowd was going to organize a coronation ceremony. Or maybe they sensed a storm. It seemed not a good night to cross the Sea of Galilee.

Did Jesus have to give the boat a shove to start them in the right direction? Jesus knew that struggling in a storm would be less dangerous for the disciples than staying with the wrong crowd who wanted to make Him an earthly king.

The Christian has not been promised smooth sailing over the sea of life. The Christian voyage is no pleasant little canoe trip down some gently flowing stream. Nor is it a perpetual picnic with the sun always shining. Storms do upset the calm of believers' lives, often unexpectedly in areas of health, family, job, or finances, bringing depression, discouragement, loneliness, rejection, or fear.

Soon the disciples encountered a squall. They had to struggle hard against wind and wave. They became distressed. Did the Lord know of their predicament? And this was a tempest which was in no way of their making. Sometimes we find ourselves in storms which we have not caused. No, when winds and waves begin to howl around us, we must never automatically conclude that we are suffering for our own wrongdoing. The storm may be divinely appointed.

The Disciples Were Not Forgotten by the Lord

Though the disciples didn't know where Jesus was, He knew where they were. The eye that never sleeps was fixed on that tossing craft. Even when He prayed on the mountain, they were in the hollow of His hand. One outline of the complete story reads: First, Christ apart from His disciples; second, Christ with His disciples. But the truth is—He was never really away from them. Artists have often painted the two parts of the story separately: the disciples bobbing in the midst of the sea, and Jesus alone on the hill praying. What should be portrayed is one composite painting in which the Saviour, from His elevated vantage point on the hill, prays and watches His beloved disciples struggling against the storm.

The Christian who finds himself in the midst of tempestuous trials can rest in the assurance that the Lord is never out of the picture but is watching over him. When meat-packing magnate Philip Armour was a young man, a banker called, saying, "I'm worried about your loan at our bank." Armour replied,

"No use both of us worrying over the same thing," and hung up.

A bishop had trouble sleeping one night as he worried over the spiritual state of the 50 churches under his jurisdiction. When the clock struck midnight, he seemed to hear a voice: "Now go to bed, Bishop. I'll sit up the rest of the night."

The temporal withdrawals of Jesus from His disciples were preparing them for the day when they would have to get along without Him. Yet He would be with them spiritually and able to assist them in every storm. Peter learned this lesson well. Years later, in prison and scheduled for execution the next morning, he was able to sleep so soundly that an angel had to hit him on the side in order to awaken him. Whenever a trial is raging, the eyes of the Lord run to and fro throughout the whole earth to show Himself strong in behalf of those who are His (see 2 Chron. 16:9).

The Disciples Did Not Receive Help Immediately

Jesus didn't come to the disciples the minute they found themselves in the storm. Jesus didn't come to Bethany the moment after receiving news of Lazarus' serious illness. He remained two days where He was, giving Lazarus time to die. He could have come at once to Mary and Martha but didn't. The sisters exclaimed on His arrival, "If Thou hadst been here, my brother had not died." But Jesus had a purpose in His delay—He wanted to perform the greater miracle of resurrection.

In a similar manner, Jesus delayed coming to the disciples. Perhaps it was as late as 9 P.M. when He ordered His disciples into the boat. But it wasn't till the fourth watch that He came (between 3 and 6 A.M.), and the headwind was so strong that they rowed only about three miles, or about a half mile an hour (Matt. 14:25; John 6:19). Since they were in the midst of the sea, it would have taken another six hours to reach the opposite shore, if in the meantime they hadn't capsized. At least four of the disciples were seasoned sailors who made their livelihood on the sea. They knew how to handle a boat in rough waters. Now as the waves rose high, tossing their boat like a piece of cork, they realized that they were in trouble—unless something happened.

119

Doubtless they remembered that earlier occasion when such a fierce storm had arisen that they had concluded all was lost. But on that occasion Jesus had been on board, though asleep, which had revealed two things about Him: His exhaustion and His trustfulness. He had been so tired that He could sleep in a violent storm with the boat rolling and pitching. And He had been so trustful of His Heavenly Father's watchcare. No novices at this sailing business, the disciples had done all they could before awaking Him. At their wits' end, and in abject fear, they had cried out for His help. Standing majestically, He had rebuked the raging elements. Immediately the storm had ceased, the winds had gone howling back to their mountainous caverns, and stillness had prevailed. "Storm, be muzzled," the Lord of Creation had ordered. The disciples had learned that He holds the whole world in His hand.

But that occasion was different. Then He had been in the boat with them. Now He was somewhere back up in the hills praying. Then He had acted the minute they sought His help. Now six hours had elapsed without His help. The storm was unabating. But they needed to grasp another lesson. Though He was miles away physically, yet He was present spiritually, watching over them all the while. Every minute of the tempest He was in complete control. They had to learn childlike faith. Two little brothers, wandering in a forest near their home, became confused and lost. When they failed to return, search parties combed the forest, finally finding them next day, unharmed and healthy. Asked what they did on learning they were lost, the older lad replied, "When it got dark, I knelt down and asked God to take care of Jimmy and me. Then we went to sleep."

The disciples doubtless thought their Master had forgotten them. As they kept bucking the headwinds midst darkness and billows, they wondered where He was. But God is never in a hurry. Omnipotence can afford to wait. Though their Master did not come immediately, He did come in His time.

The Disciples Got Help in an Unexpected Way

Who would have expected Jesus to come using water as pave-

ment for His approach? He used the very waves that threatened to swallow them, showing His mastery over the frightful
elements. He often tramples on the very experience we're
passing through. Hymnist William Cowper put it,

> God moves in a mysterious way
> His wonders to perform;
> He plants His footsteps in the sea
> And rides upon the storm.

The disciples may have figured out how they wanted their
Master to rescue them, but He came His own way. Suddenly,
midst all the strain and agonizing, it happened. Facing the
direction from which they had come, with backs to the wind,
suddenly through the darkness and foam, they caught a
glimpse of a figure moving majestically toward them, walking
on the frothy, mountainous waves, rising and falling, always on
top of them, defying the law of gravity. Unimpeded, He
walked straight into the gale, so fast He was catching up and
was about to pass alongside the boat. In the midst of their
confusion, yelling at each other what to do, they all saw Him.
Alarmed, they cried out, "A ghost!" These rough, tough men
were used to fighting storms. But when they saw what appeared to be a ghostly figure stepping on water, they weren't
used to that. They did not know who it was since they did not
expect Jesus to work in this way. Perhaps seeing the appari-
tion may have been worse than the storm. They wanted rescue but not this unexplainable form. They did not recognize
Jesus in a new role, so they cried out in fear.

Often the Lord comes to us in ways we would never expect.
The woman of Samaria, having suffered the stress of several
marriage breakups, plus a current immoral affair, never imagined on her way at noon to draw water from the well that she
would meet the One who would quench the spiritual thirst
burning in her soul. Or that He would make her an evangelist
to her people. When the repentant thief was cruelly nailed to a
Roman gibbet that Good Friday morn, little did he realize that
before noon he would come to believe in the Victim on the

middle cross and hear Him say, "Today shalt thou be with Me in paradise." What a glorious, unexpected reversal of storm. He started the day as a condemned thief, facing crucifixion, without hope in this life or in the world to come, and ended the day with Christ in paradise.

The Philippian jailer at one moment was about to commit suicide because he thought his prisoners had escaped. But an hour later, as a new believer, in joy he washed the prisoners' backs, soothed their stripes, provided food for their bodies, and was baptized with the rest of his household. His storm had subsided and in such an unexpected way—through an earthquake.

When a plant closed down on Long Island, an electronics engineer was unable to find work. He sent his resumé to company after company, but without success. Too proud to tell parents or relatives of their precarious financial status, the couple was down to their last can of noodle soup. As was their custom, they bowed their heads and prayed the Lord's Prayer. The husband loved to eat bread with soup but today there was no bread. With great deliberation the couple uttered, "Give us this day our daily bread." Just then came a persistent knocking at the back door. They hurried through the rest of the prayer; then the wife answered the door.

The husband heard a neighbor's voice say, "Can you use any bread? My brother is a route man for one of the big companies. They've been having an advertising campaign, giving out sample loaves. He was given more than he needed for his stores. He has four cases left. He can't bring the cases back because the bread has to be fresh each day. I've taken two cases and can't fit any more in my house. Can you use the other two?"

Husband and wife were astonished at the immediacy and sufficiency of the answer. After the caller left, they praised God for bread in the breadbox, bread in the refrigerator, bread in the freezer, and bread on the table. Shortly thereafter, the husband was able to find work, but they always thanked God for their serendipity experience midst the storm of unemployment.

The Disciples' Fear Was Dispelled

As the disciples cried out in fear, Jesus identified Himself, calling out, "Be of good cheer; it is I: be not afraid." What an unnatural announcement if He were only man. What a natural statement if He were truly God. Before taking them out of the storm, He took the storm out of them. To have calm in the storm, we must recognize Jesus as Master of the universe. The ancient symbol of impossibility was the figure of two feet planted on a fragment of ocean. By making water a pavement and walking on it, Jesus proved Himself the God of the impossible. Though Jesus usually traveled by land, in this miracle He traveled by sea without the use of a boat, and in the Ascension by air without an airplane.

As soon as Jesus identified Himself, Peter, overwhelmed by this demonstration of power, called out, "Lord, if it be Thou, bid me come unto Thee on the water." How wonderful that, like Peter, we can talk to the Lord midst the storms of life! Why did Peter make such a request? Not because he wanted to pull some stunt but rather because impulsively he wished to get closer to Christ, which meant leaving the boat.

Jesus didn't discourage him, but simply said, "Come." Peter started out magnificently. Climbing out of the boat, he walked on the water toward Jesus. Up to the top of a wave with all its foam Peter went, then down the other side into the hollow, and back up the next wave. Then his eyes wandered from Jesus to the waves, and he began to sink. He cried out a short prayer, "Lord, save me." Had Peter prayed the average pastoral prayer, he likely would have been at the bottom of the lake before he finished. Immediately, Jesus stretched forth His hand, rescuing Peter, who walked with Jesus back to the boat.

Jesus' rebuke to Peter for his little faith was an indirect acknowledgment of some faith on Peter's part. Peter actually walked on water, even if only a few feet. No other disciple showed such trust then. Only Peter took steps of faith to walk a bridge over troubled waters. With humility he could say, "I walked on water. I experienced the sensation of buoyancy over tossing waves." This experience would help them all face later storms. As they went from council to council, from prison to prison, from trial to trial, they would also go from faith to faith.

In the boat with them Christ's presence brought deeper calm. Today the Lord can enter the ship of your life in His good time, stilling the storm and bringing His cheer. The record also says that immediately the boat reached the shore where they were headed. Many expositors believe another miracle took place—the sudden traversing of the distance from midlake to land. The story may contain four possible miracles: Jesus walking on the waves; His causing Peter to walk on water; His power to still the storm; and His conquest of space for the boat to be immediately at land.

Storms: A Picture of Troubles

Old Testament metaphors make the restless sea a symbol of danger, terror, and a troubled conscience (Isa. 57:20). The psalmist portrays Jehovah's authority over wind and wave. He speaks of "the stormy wind, which lifteth up the waves thereof. They mount up to the heaven, they go down again to the depths, for their soul is melted because of trouble. They reel to and fro, and stagger like a drunken man, and are at their wit's end. Then they cry unto the Lord in their trouble, and He bringeth them out of their distresses. He maketh the storm a calm, so that the waves thereof are still. Then are they glad because they be quiet; so He bringeth them unto their desired haven" (Ps. 107:25-30). These verses seem like a poetic description, centuries in advance, of this miracle of the stilling of the storm.

Our placid lake of life can suddenly turn into a churning storm of temptation, anxiety, illness, suffering, tragedy, job loss, financial reverse, or pending death. According to a Finnish engineer, after Finnish troops recaptured a town from the Russian army during World War II, seven Red prisoners were sentenced to be shot at dawn on Monday. On Sunday the atmosphere was tempestuous. The Finnish soldiers, standing guard with their rifles, taunted the seven prisoners held in the basement of the town hall, who swore repeatedly and beat the walls with their bloodied fists. Some prisoners pathetically called for their wives and children who were far away.

Then something happened late that night. One of the condemned men began to sing! Some soldiers exclaimed, "He's mad!" The engineer had noticed that this man, Koshkinen, had not raved and sworn like the others. Quietly he had sat on his bench, a picture of utter despair. As he began to sing, no one said anything to him. His voice, wavering at first, grew stronger. All the prisoners turned and looked at the singer who seemed to be in his element as he sang:

Safe in the arms of Jesus, safe on His gentle breast,
There by His love o'ershadowed, sweetly my soul shall
    rest.
Hark, 'tis the voice of angels, borne in a song to me,
Over the fields of glory, over the jasper sea.

Repeatedly, Koshkinen sang that verse. When he stopped, all were quiet for a few minutes till a wild-looking prisoner yelled, "Where did you get that, you fool? Are you trying to make us religious?" With tears in his eyes, Koshkinen answered, "I got this song from The Salvation Army. I heard it there three weeks ago. At first I laughed at it, but it got to me. It's cowardly to hide your beliefs. The God my mother believed in has now become my God also. As I lay awake last night, I felt that I had to find the Saviour and hide in Him. Then I prayed like the thief on the cross that Christ would forgive me, cleanse my sinful soul, and make me ready to stand before Him whom I should soon meet. Verses from the Bible and old hymns came to my mind. They brought a message of pardon from the crucified Saviour. I thanked Him. Since then this hymn has been sounding inside me. I could no longer keep it to myself. In a few hours I shall be with the Lord, saved by His grace."

Koshkinen's face shone. The Finnish soldiers listened to what the Russian had to say. Then one of Koshkinen's comrades moaned, "If only I knew that there is mercy for me too! But these hands of mine have shed blood, and I've reviled God and trampled on all that's holy, and I deserve hell." He sank to the ground in despair. He begged Koshkinen to pray for him. And there these two Red soldiers went down on their knees. The Finnish soldiers forgot their hatred. By 4 o'clock Monday morning all Koshkinen's comrades had begun to pray. The change in the atmosphere was indescribable. Though day was dawning, no one had had a moment's sleep. "Sing the song once more for us, Koshkinen," said one of them. And how they sang! Not only that song but verses and choruses long forgotten came forth from their memories. The Finnish soldiers, though on guard, united their voices with them.

The town clock struck 6. The guards wished they could have begged for mercy for these men, but knew this was impossible. Between two rows of guards the Russians marched to execution. One asked to be allowed to sing Koshkinen's song once more. Permission was granted. Then they asked to die with uncovered faces. With hands raised to heaven they sang with all their strength, "Safe in the arms of Jesus, safe on His gentle breast." When the last line died out, the lieutenant gave the word, "Fire!" The seven Red soldiers went singing into heaven, having fought their last fight. The guards bowed their heads in silent prayer. Said one guard, "What happened in the hearts of others I do not know, but I was a new man from that hour." He had seen men facing the terror of impending death. Then he had seen Christ still the storm as they looked to Him who has dominion over the sea (*The Salvation Army War Cry*).

As a motto reads, "The Lord will either calm your storm, or allow it to rage while He calms you."

ONCE I WAS BLIND
BUT NOW I CAN SEE

K arsten Ohnstad, an American high school boy, lost his eyesight through a minor sports injury. Fourteen years later he had graduated from a high school for the blind, completed college, also earned an M.A., and had authored an autobiography, *The World at My Fingertips,* later condensed in the *Reader's Digest* (September 1942), which told the story of his undaunted courage over countless obstacles.

Learning to get around indoors cost time and bruises. He smashed into a half-open bathroom door. Minutes later, walking into the kitchen, he banged headlong into the open pantry door. His mother suggested, "Put your hand in front of you when you walk." However, Karsten preferred the bruises to the embarrassment of walking around with extended hands.

Grabbing for objects which slipped from his hands was a habit difficult to break. Table corners and chair arms, often in the way, shattered his dark glasses or grazed his cheek as he attempted to retrieve a coin or piece of paper. He slowly learned to wait till the fallen object had stopped moving. Eating salad was particularly trying because of unmanageable lettuce leaves. At a neighbor's for dinner, Karsten heard a six-year-old boy comment, "Look! His fork ain't got nothin' on it!"

Walking outside, he often failed to turn at the right moment and found himself straddling a prickly hedge, trampling a rose-bush, or stumbling into a woodpile. But one day he discovered he could determine the presence and size of nearby objects, such as buildings and trees, by snapping his fingers and listen-ing to the type of echo. Busy street corners were almost impossible, and he strained his ears to estimate his chances of reaching the other side. Eventually, swallowing pride, Karsten used a cane, and suddenly became "Moses of the Metropolis," able to hold out his staff, part the traffic, and walk safely to the other side.

When he began to master Braille, the tip of his finger be-came sore, then numb, from sliding over line after line of dots. Often Karsten returned a new, sharply dotted book to the library with blood on its pages.

Blindness must be very difficult. *The American Foundation for the Blind* in New York City estimates there are 600,000 legally blind people in the United States and 2 million severely visually impaired. Anthony Campolo in *Seven Deadly Sins* says more than 100,000 children around the world go blind every year due to lack of vitamin A in their diets (Victor, 1987, p. 143).

Eastern nations in earlier centuries had a high incidence of blindness. The condition was aggravated by sand and sun glare. Flies often covered matter-encrusted eyes. Many blind lived in Jesus' time, mostly beggars, and happily, several came in contact with the great miracle worker. One of the prophe-cies concerning the promised Messiah was that He would bring sight to the blind (Luke 4:18). For John the Baptist in prison, one of the signs of Jesus' messiahship was that "the blind receive their sight" (Matt. 11:5).

We are told of Jesus healing the blind on seven occasions. Two of these deal with *people in a group*. Just before He fed the 4,000, great multitudes brought the sick to Jesus, and cast them at His feet, among them the blind. "And He healed them" (Matt. 15:30). In Jesus' final week we read that "the blind . . . came to Him in the temple; and He healed them" (Matt. 21:14).

The other five cures of blindness involve *specific individuals,* and in this probable chronological order:
—the blind and dumb demoniac in Galilee (Matt. 12:22);
—two blind men in Galilee (Matt. 9:27-31);
—the man born blind in Jerusalem (John 9);
—the blind man at Bethsaida (Mark 7:22-26);
—Bartimaeus and an unnamed companion at Jericho (Matt. 20:29-34; Mark 10:46-52; Luke 18:35-43).

We shall take a look at the last three of these.

The Man Born Blind Healed in Jerusalem
One day Jesus was moved by the sight of a blind beggar, perhaps sitting near the temple gate to capitalize on the piety of departing worshipers (John 9). Many delights were denied him, like the glory of a sunset and the sight of his mother's face. Among the Gospel miracles, this is the only sufferer whose malady is mentioned as present from birth.

Noting the Master's interest in the victim, the disciples asked, "Who did sin, this man, or his parents, that he was born blind?" Some, then, believed that sins committed in a previous existence resulted in illnesses in this life. Jesus answered that neither this man nor his parents had sinned but he was born blind so that a divine work might be displayed through this man, thus bringing glory to God. Speculation on the relation of people's sickness to their sins might be a convenient way to neglect the disabled. The disciples were philosophizing when they should have been philanthropizing. But compassionate Jesus said, "The night cometh, when no man can work," then sprang into action. Uttering an affirmation appropriate to a blind man's condition, "I am the Light of the world," Jesus spat on the ground, made mud with His saliva, put it on the man's eyes, and told him to go wash in the pool of Siloam. The blind man began to ambulate toward the pool, his eyes covered with mud, his heart pounding. Washing his eyes, suddenly he could see!

● *His neighbors.* Remarkable were the reactions of others, especially neighbors and Pharisees. The neighbors weren't quite sure this was the same man they had seen sitting begging day after day. But the healed man insisted, "I am the one!" Wouldn't you think they would have thrown a party to celebrate the joy of this man who kept repeating, "I can see! I can see!" Instead, they asked how his eyes were opened. When he responded directly, the neighbors were nonplussed, for they had never heard of such a thing. So they brought the healed man to the Pharisees.

● *The Pharisees.* Then follow three laughable cross-examinations by the Pharisees: first, they questioned the blind man, then his parents, then again the blind man. To stand before this austere council in their chambers must have been awesome. Yet subtle humor pervades these dialogues as the dignity of the Pharisees is ruffled in their attempt to prove the miracle never happened. Incidentally, this may be the best attested of Jesus' miracles from the standpoint of intense official investigation.

In the first interview the Pharisees, who majored in minors and minored in majors, pounced on the fact that Jesus made clay on the Sabbath, while forgetting His compassionate act. They cared more for their man-made regulations than for people. Some concluded that because of this Sabbath violation Jesus could not be of God. But others asked how a sinful man could do such wonders. The Pharisees turned to the blind man for his opinion. In the rapture of his new sight, he answered that Jesus must have been more than mere man—a prophet at least.

In the hope of finding some discrepancy in the blind man's story, the Pharisees called in his parents. Intimidated lest they be excommunicated from the synagogue, they passed the buck back to their son: "He is of age; ask him."

So, interrogating the son again, the Pharisees urged him to give honor to God but not to Jesus, whom they called a sinner. The son pointed out that whatever they thought of Jesus, He did open his eyes. The cornered Pharisees called for a second

recital of the facts of his healing, hoping to find some contra-
diction. But the healed man refused to believe Jesus was a
sinner. Becoming impatient with their failure to accept the
facts, he turned the tables on them with relentless logic. He
pointed out that it was astonishing that they didn't know anything about this man who had the power to heal the blind. He
concluded, "If this man were not of God, He could do
nothing."

At this point the Pharisees, who had already reviled the
man, insulted him by saying, "How dare you who were born in
sin teach us who are your professors!" Then they excommunicated him.

● *Found by Jesus.* Ejected by the religious leaders, the man
with restored sight was not cast out by Christ. The seeking
Saviour, hearing what had happened, found him and revealed
Himself as the Son of God. Then the man confessed, "Lord, I
believe," and worshiped Jesus. He had experienced the power
of the Lord; now he knew the Person.

The Spiritually Blind

Physical blindness is a type of spiritual blindness. In our natural estate we cannot see spiritual truth. But Jesus came to give
spiritual sight to the spiritually blind. After the healing of the
blind man, Jesus commented, "For judgment I am come into
this world, that they which see not might see; and that they
which see might be made blind." He meant that those who
humbly admitted their spiritual ignorance could become the
recipients of spiritual insight, whereas those who were filled
with their own self-knowledge would remain in their blindness.
A proverb puts it, "There are none so blind as those who will
not see."

Some of the Pharisees then asked Jesus, "Are we blind
also?" He answered in effect, "If you would admit your need of
light, you would receive enlightenment. But since you claim to
see when you are really blind, you remain in your sin" (9:41).
A poet tells of his pity for a blind man walking with a cane.
Speaking with him, the poet began to realize that the blind man

131

THE MIRACLES OF JESUS

possessed far greater insight than he, concluding with, "I, not he, was blind."

● *Blind to the simplicity of the Gospel.* Paul wrote of the lost, "The god of this world hath blinded the minds of them which believe not, lest the light of the glorious Gospel of Christ . . . should shine unto them" (2 Cor. 4:4). Jesus spoke of "blind leaders of the blind" (Matt. 15:14).

Spiritually blind people cannot see their need of salvation, nor understand how someone dying on a cross can atone for their sins, nor can they grasp salvation as a free gift apart from human merit. When an open-air preacher in Hyde Park, London, finished a Gospel testimony, a man stepped from the crowd saying, "Ladies and gentlemen, you've been listening to this chap talking about God, Jesus Christ, sin, death, heaven, and hell. Don't believe a word of it. I don't. I refuse to believe what I cannot see."

When he finished, another man elbowed his way to the front. "Friends, I hear that not far from here runs a river. I don't believe it. Many say the grass around is a lovely green. I don't believe it. I'm told that pretty flowers abound around here. I don't believe it. Many of you will think I'm talking like a fool. But I am serious. I have never seen the river. I have never seen the grass, nor the flowers, for I was born blind. Unless sight is given me I shall never see these things. But does that allow me to insist that what I cannot see I will not believe? Certainly not!" Turning toward the agnostic, the blind man continued. "You, sir, by your statements, disprove nothing that has been said. What you do prove is that you are blind—spiritually blind—and that's why you do not understand what many here know to be true."

● *Blind to our own spiritual immaturity.* Peter lists a series of virtues which every believer should possess, then warns, "He that lacketh these things is blind, and cannot see afar off, and hath forgotten that he was purged from his old sins" (2 Peter 1:9). Blind indeed is the professing believer who neglects to cultivate the Christian graces.

● *Blind to divine perspective.* Visual agnosia, a neurological disorder which prevents seeing a scene as a whole, causes a victim to identify some details about a friend's face, such as his big nose or trimmed mustache, but prevents him from recognizing the friend when shown a picture of his complete face. Individual features of a landscape may be noted but not the view as a unit. Often our spiritual eyes jump from detail to detail but fail to put everything in perspective.

The Pharisees were suffering from spiritual agnosia when they would rather that a man remain blind than have their man-made Sabbath regulation violated. They could see only the detail of their little rule, while missing the bigger picture of love and care for a man born blind. They strained out gnats from their cup, while agnosia-like, they swallowed camels (v. 24).

● *Blind to our own faults.* A California woman became very agitated by the continuous, hacking cough of her pet parrot. A vet examined the bird and pronounced it perfectly healthy. The parrot had merely learned to imitate the raspy bark of its cigarette-smoking owner. Jesus warned against taking a sliver out of a brother's eye while at the same time a piece of lumber protrudes from our own. His remedy: first get the piece of lumber out of our eye; then we will see clearly to pick out the speck from our brother's.

UPI newsman Wes Pippert tells of a press conference held by Jody Powell, the fun-loving, combative press secretary, the night before former President Carter's inauguration. Powell was briefing reporters on Carter's inaugural address, in which he quoted the Prophet Micah about doing justly. Having a strong church background, Powell asked with a twinkle in his eye, "OK, what prophets precede and follow Micah?" Despite his M.A. in Old Testament from Wheaton College, Pippert couldn't recall for sure. When one reporter suggested Jeremiah, Powell said smugly, "Wrong." Taking a deep breath, he recited, "Hosea, Joel, Amos, Obadiah, Jonah, Micah, Nahum, Habakkuk, Zephaniah, Haggai, Zechariah, Malachi," then grinned.

Some time later Powell called the *Chicago Sun-Times* to spread a damaging but groundless rumor about Senator Charles Percy who then was presiding over the Burt Lance Senate hearings. Though Lance's actions may have been questionable, Pippert said that "Powell's action was qualitatively worse in that he set out to damage, if not to destroy, a person." Pippert later confronted Powell on the matter. Powell replied indifferently, "Well, isn't this the way it's done in Washington?" Said Pippert, "It was a grim scene. Jody Powell knew the names of the minor prophets, but he had not brought the message of the minor prophets to bear on every part of his life."

● *Blinded by money.* A coin as small as a penny held close to the eye can blot out the sun. Money can keep us from seeing truth and justice. The Old Testament warns against letting a gift blind the wise (Ex. 23:8; Deut. 16:19; 1 Sam. 12:3).

Jack Eckerd, founder of the Eckerd drugstore chain, became a Christian in 1983. Soon afterward, walking through one of his stores, though he had looked at the magazine racks a thousand times before, this time *he saw with new eyes* the pornographic magazines for sale there. He called his company president and ordered him to remove *Playboy* and *Penthouse*. The president was stunned because those magazines brought in several million dollars in profit annually. Eckerd insisted. Those magazines were cleared from the shelves of the 1,700 Eckerd drugstores. He was simply yielding to the lordship of Christ. "Why else would I throw a few million dollars out of the window?" He would not let money blind him.

● *Blinded by hate.* John wrote, "He that hateth his brother is in darkness, and walketh in darkness, and knoweth not whither he goeth, because that darkness hath blinded his eyes" (1 John 2:11). To hold a grudge against a fellow believer is evidence of blindness.

● *The blindness of halfheartedness.* To the lukewarm

134

church at Laodicea came this admonition, "Because thou sayest, I am rich, and increased with goods, and have need of nothing; and knowest not that thou art wretched, and miserable, and poor, and blind, and naked: I counsel thee to . . . anoint thine eyes with eye salve, that thou mayest see" (Rev. 3:17-18).

Whether a person is blind because he never understood the Gospel, or blind as a believer because he was deceived by the love of money or by the cares of this world, that person needs the miracle of spiritual sight.

A Blind Man Needing a Second Touch

A man who was losing his sight said his biggest fear was losing his ability to support his family. With his eyes getting progressively worse, he didn't know where to turn. That's when the Lighthouse, an organization also known as the New York Association for the Blind, which since 1906 has been helping the blind to cope, came to the rescue. They designed a large-print video computer that made it possible for him to keep his job. Letters which before were difficult for him to make out now became clear.

The healing of a blind man brought to Jesus at Bethsaida is the only recorded gradual miracle in the Gospels (Mark 8:22-25). After leading the blind man by the hand out of the city, Jesus spat on his eyes. Putting His hands on him, Jesus asked if he saw anything. The man replied that he saw men as trees walking. At this first stage vision was restored but imperfectly. Everything seemed vague. Then Jesus put His hands on him again. This time, when he looked up, he saw people clearly—a two-stage healing.

This often happens when the Lord gives spiritual sight. People reach a partway mark. They sense spiritual realities never before realized, though to them spiritual truth remains still somewhat vague. Their vision needs clarification through growth in grace and knowledge. Jim Elliot, martyred by the Aucas, wrote in his diary that "a man does not have to come all at once into the family of God with a jolt and accompanying spinal exhilarations. Personally, I wasn't 'saved' all at once, but

135

took some years coming into my present settled convictions about the truth of God. So why should I demand that conversion be immediate in all others? Christ healed men differently. . . . He spoke a word, and there was a lightning-fast reaction. Others He touched, spat upon, made clay, spoke to and questioned, then when they saw men 'as trees walking' He went through the whole process again. Let not him who accepts light in an instant despise him who gropes months in shadows. . . . The natural, so often illustrative of the spiritual, teaches that healing and growth, yea, even birth, are processes, and I think we altar-callers often perform abortions in our haste to see 'results'" (Elisabeth Elliot, *Shadow of the Almighty,* Harper, 1958, pp. 77–78).

Hearing the testimonies of how people became Christians is always interesting but also risky. For the hearer, the danger exists of doubting his own conversion if it hasn't happened much the same way as the testifier's. He hears statements such as: "On May 1, exactly at 9:20 P.M., I accepted Christ" /"I was there when it happened, so I know it's real"/"All desire for alcohol and dope disappeared immediately, and I've never touched either from that day on"/"I've never had a single doubt since."

For the testifier the danger may be rejecting the conversion of all others whose story isn't precisely identical to his. One deacon who had mourned months over his sins tended to be hard on prospective church members who hadn't gone through at least a three-month period of deep conviction. Imagine three of the blind men healed by Jesus getting together for a praise service. One says, "He put mud on my eyes." The second says, "He just touched me." The third says, "He both put mud on my eyes and touched me twice." They began to argue among themselves as to who was really healed. Unable to agree, they started separate churches: the Mudites, the Touchites, and the Two Touchites.

God is the God of variety. Though there's only one way to the Father, which is through Jesus Christ, there are as many ways to Jesus as there are people. Each conversion is a unique story. In Acts, Saul was converted dramatically; Lydia came to

Christ quietly. Saul was converted at midday; the jailer, at midnight. The Ethiopian eunuch was riding in a chariot; the jailer was in a prison complex; Lydia was by a river. Some would say that Apollos was a half-Christian when he came to Ephesus, where he entered into full spiritual vision; both Paul and the jailer received spiritual sight in sudden, dramatic fashion.

Dr. Donald Grey Barnhouse wrote that when seven or eight years of age he was moved to tears at a Gospel sermon and walked an aisle to take the evangelist by the hand. Then he remembered how at 15 he became aware of the sinfulness of his heart and was pointed to appropriate Bible verses by a faithful man. For several years as he grew rapidly in the faith he would point to the age-15 experience as the time of his conversion. But he came to this conclusion: "I know now, of course, that I was wrong. All that happened to me when I was 15 was that I became aware of the possession of the eternal life which had been given to me by God long before then" (*Epistle to the Romans*, Evangelical Foundation, *Booklet 37*, pp. 1799–1800).

This two-stage miracle teaches how patient the Lord is with our slowness to learn. The healed man did not perceive men clearly at first, but later, after a second touch, they suddenly were in sharp focus. If you perceive spiritual truth faintly, use every means of grace to let the Lord give you clearer sight.

Blind Bartimaeus at Jericho

Matthew reports that Jesus healed two blind men at this time, whereas Mark and Luke focus on just one (see Matt. 20:29-34; Mark 10:46-52; Luke 18:35-43). Mark calls the man in his account Bartimaeus; this is one of the few reports of miracles in which a name is given.

He was a blind beggar, dependent on someone to lead him each day to a spot beside the highway where, along with other beggars, he would keep calling out for charity. Though he had lost his sight, he had not lost his hearing. He had heard of other blind men Jesus of Nazareth had healed. Unable to search for Jesus, he hoped that someday Jesus would come by

Jericho. Then it happened. One day an unusually large crowd approached. Straining to hear, he asked what it meant. Came the answer, "Jesus of Nazareth is passing by." Immediately he began to yell, "Thou Son of David, have mercy on me!" Perhaps his use of Jesus' messianic title indicated his faith in Jesus as the Christ.

What stands out is the beggar's sheer determination. Unlike the other two cases, here the initiative came from Bartimaeus. No one suggested that he call out to Jesus. On the contrary, bystanders told him to shut up, "but he called out all the more."

Jesus stood still and commanded that the blind man be brought to him. Bartimaeus threw off his cloak and, jumping up, was led to Jesus, who asked, "What do you want Me to do for you?" Bartimaeus might have wondered if Jesus too were blind. Could He not see his clouded eyes, his beggar's cup, and his uncertain gait? Then his ears caught the strength of Jesus' words which were not meant to tease him, but to encourage. Bartimaeus replied, "Lord, that I may receive my sight."

Jesus replied, "Receive thy sight: thy faith hath saved thee." Immediately Bartimaeus received his sight, and followed Jesus, glorifying God. What a thrill to see! A woman who had had an eye operation told me, "I went all to pieces when I saw the doctor's fingers and could count them. I could see the window shades. I just lost control of myself!" When the beggar received his sight, he saw the face of Jesus, then the crowd, then palm trees, the walls of Jericho, and the mountain of Moab. No wonder he glorified God. That same voice which had begged so loudly for mercy now boomed forth great volumes of praise. He also joined the large crowd following Jesus on this final stage of His last journey to Jerusalem. His praise was contagious, for the people seeing the miracle also gave praise to God. His receiving physical sight pictures the possibility of our receiving spiritual vision and of seeing things in a new way. Also, much as a doctor receives great gratification in restoring a person's vision, so we experience delight in aiding someone to find spiritual insight.

ONCE I WAS BLIND BUT NOW I CAN SEE

In 1961, at age eight, Prayat, a Thai boy, became blind through a car accident. Soon afterward he was expelled from school by a teacher who said, "You can't read the blackboard, so don't come." Frustrated at every attempt to get an education, finally at 15 he entered a vocational training center for the blind to learn carpentry. Becoming a Christian and wishing to help others, he was admitted to night school after seven unsuccessful attempts, going on to graduate from a teacher's training college. With a burden for the thousands of visually handicapped, Prayat went to northeast Thailand in 1978 with $500 to begin a training school for the blind. Renting a house, he used half the building for a school. Six children and seven adults moved in with Prayat as their teacher.

Despite skepticism and resistance, more than 100 students have benefited from his school, learning survival skills such as feeding themselves and moving independently. They attend public schools as soon as possible, and with Braille textbooks and a tutor can keep up with sighted classmates. Since Thailand was not producing any Braille books, through World Concern the school, known as the Christian Foundation for the Blind, now has Braille typewriters and produces Braille textbooks for all 12 grades. Also available is a Braille Bible plus devotional materials, so that the blind receive not only physical help but have the Gospel in their own language.

Prayat's favorite Gospel song is "Amazing Grace," especially the line, "I . . . was blind, but now I see."

A FIG
TREE CURSED

Roger would never forget the date—May 7. Just released from the Army, he was hitchhiking home. To his surprise a black, sleek, new Cadillac stopped. He learned that the driver whose name was Hanover had a business in Chicago and would be driving near the soldier's home. After talking about many things, Roger, a Christian, felt compelled to witness to this middle-aged, prosperous businessman. Putting it off as long as he could, he cleared his throat and explained the way of salvation. As Hanover pulled the car to the side of the road, Roger thought he was about to be asked to get out. But the businessman bowed his head, received Christ, and thanked Roger, declaring, "This is the greatest day of my life."

Five years later Roger, on a trip to Chicago, found the business card Hanover had given him five years before and decided to visit him. Ushered into a beautiful office, Roger faced a keen-eyed, middle-aged woman. She extended her hand saying, "You knew my husband?"

Roger told how her husband had given him a ride home.

"Can you tell me when that was?" she asked.

He replied, "It was May 7, five years ago, the day I was discharged from the Army."

"Anything special about that day?" she asked.

After momentary hesitation, Roger decided to tell her about his witness. "Mrs. Hanover, I explained the Gospel to him. He pulled over to the side of the road and wept against the steering wheel as he accepted Christ that afternoon."

Explosive sobs shook her body. "I had prayed for my husband's salvation for years. I had believed God would save him."

"And where is your husband now, Mrs. Hanover?"

"He's dead. He was in a car crash after he let you out. He never got home." Sobbing uncontrollably, she added, "I stopped living for God five years ago because I thought He had not answered my prayer."

For five years this widow had lived an unproductive Christian life. To warn against fruitlessness in the believer's walk, Jesus performed a miracle causing a fig tree to wither. It happened on the Monday after the so-called Triumphal Entry of Palm Sunday. On His way to Jerusalem, after spending the night in Bethany, perhaps in the home of Mary, Martha, and Lazarus, Jesus was approaching the city when He noticed a fig tree. Its luxuriant leaves, visible at a distance, gave promise that figs would also be found thereon, even though not yet the season. But finding only leaves and no fruit, Jesus pronounced a death sentence on the tree. Immediately it began the decaying process. Next day the disciples, again passing that way, were amazed to find that the tree had withered right from its roots. The story is told in Matthew 21:18-22 and Mark 11:12-14, 20-26.

Unlikely Miracle

Of all Jesus' miracles this one has raised the most questions and is the least understood; it is just the reverse of His first nature miracle. Then He used power to bless a wedding by changing water into wine, thus preventing the bride and groom from suffering great embarrassment. In contrast to the benevolent cheer of that festive occasion, His mood is now severe and malevolent, as He curses a tree. It seems so out of character with the rest of His miracles, a mere conjurer's trick to show power seemingly devoid of reason and morality.

On the surface this miracle puts Jesus in a bad light. How unlike the One who at the beginning of His ministry refused to turn stones into bread to satisfy His hunger. And now in His final week He blasts a fig tree because it does not contain fruit to satisfy His hunger! Furthermore, He curses it for not having fruit at Passover, a time not the season for figs. Why does He curse a soulless, nonvolitional, nonpersonal entity, not responsible for its fruitlessness.

Dr. Donald Grey Barnhouse said that when he picked figs as a boy in California he missed some concealed under large leaves. He recalled that "it was typical for me to find fresh figs in July and August, perhaps a few in September, and then, when the leaves fell off, to find dry figs in October and November, still on the tree. It was perfectly possible and plausible for Jesus to look for some of those dried figs, still on the tree from the season past, amid the first green leaves of the new crop to come" (*Mark: The Servant Gospel,* Victor Books, p. 108). Even if He expected to find premature fruit or dried figs still hanging there from an earlier season, imagine Jesus showing irritation at a senseless object in no way at fault!

The key to this miracle's interpretation must be found in its symbolism. When people would not listen to their words, Old Testament prophets dramatized their message vividly for people to see. One day Ahijah stopped Jeroboam when they were alone in a field outside Jerusalem, ripped his own new robe into 12 pieces, handed Jeroboam 10 and kept 2. This visually portrayed the splitting of the kingdom of Israel, with 10 of the tribes given to Jeroboam to rule (1 Kings 11:29-32). New Testament prophet Agabus, meeting Paul at Caesarea, took the apostle's belt and bound his own hands to graphically predict that if Paul continued on his journey to Rome, he would end up a prisoner (Acts 21:10-11). So the cursing of the fig tree was not merely a horticultural sentence on a fruitless tree. Jesus' action was a symbolic pronouncement of doom on Israel.

Warning against Judaism

The fig tree was the best known and loved tree in the Holy Land. Though it grew to a height of only 15 to 20 feet, its branches spread from 25 to 35 feet, making it valuable not only for its fruit but for its shade.

Israel is often spoken of as a fig tree in the Old Testament. In this miracle the large leaves represent the empty traditions and ceremonies by which God's people often tried to cover up the nakedness of their spiritual life, just as Adam and Eve attempted to conceal their nakedness with fig leaves after partaking of the forbidden fruit. The fig tree represents God's people who had received more privileges than any other group in the world. But repeatedly they had turned their backs on His blessings, while still maintaining an outward show of piety. Though they drew near Him with their mouths, their hearts were far from Him. Their pretense turned out to be leaves without figs.

In the Book of Isaiah, God speaks of Israel as a vineyard: "My beloved had a vineyard on a very fertile hill. He digged it and cleared it of stones, and planted it with choice vines; He built a watchtower in the midst of it, and hewed out a wine vat in it; and He looked for it to yield grapes, but it yielded wild grapes. . . . And now I will tell you what I will do to My vineyard. . . . I will make it a waste. . . . For the vineyard of the Lord of hosts is the house of Israel, and the men of Judah are His pleasant planting" (Isa. 5:1-7, RSV). Jeremiah links the two images of grapes and figs: " 'I will surely consume them,' saith the Lord; 'there shall be no grapes on the vine, nor figs on the fig tree, and the leaf shall fade; and the things that I have given them shall pass away from them' " (8:13). God wanted good grapes from His vine, and good figs from His fig tree but all He found were sour grapes and no figs. So through the prophets God pronounced a curse on the nation, which Jesus then reinforced by an acted parable, the cursing of the fig tree.

When Jesus came to earth, official Judaism—the Sanhedrin, the Sadducees, and the Pharisees—were all barren fig trees in God's sight. They also aggravated their fruitlessness by an

143

outward show of piety, strict Sabbath observance, adherence to oral tradition, and an elaborate parade of sacrifices. Then on Palm Sunday the people made a great show of welcome to Jesus, crying out their Hosannas and strewing palm branches in His way as He rode triumphantly into Jerusalem on a donkey. But in a few days the same crowd would scream, "Crucify Him!"

The focal point of the leaders' hypocrisy was the temple in Jerusalem. Income from temple worship generated a flow of coins into the coffers of the religious elite. The money changers charged a fee for exchanging common coins for acceptable money. Merchants sold sheep for sacrifices to pilgrims coming from a distance. Those living nearby often had their animals rejected, requiring them to buy a sheep from the temple merchants at an inflated price. The house of prayer had degenerated into a bank and a lucrative cattle market crowded with tables and reeking with the stench of manure. Outraged at the perversion of His Father's house into a den of thieves, Jesus "began to cast out them that sold and bought in the temple, and overthrew the tables of the money changers, and the seats of them that sold doves" (Mark 11:15). Striking at the most venerated spot in the Holy Land, Jesus knew full well that His behavior would be considered blasphemy of the highest order and would hasten His death on the cross, where in the eternal plan of God He would become the perfect sacrifice, the Lamb of God, to take away the sins of the world.

Significantly, Mark relates the story of the fig tree in two parts (9:12-14 and 20-22), with the cleansing of the temple framed in between (15-19). On one day Jesus pronounced a curse on the fig tree, then later cleansed the temple; then next day the disciples noted the tree completely withered. The sandwiching of the temple cleansing between parts of the fig tree cursing shows the close association of the two events. Jesus cursed a tree which symbolized Israel and soon after struck at the very nerve center of Jewish religion. Later that week, at His death, the temple curtain which hid the holy of holies ripped from top to bottom, indicating the end of the Old Testament system. Though the curtain was patched up, the

144

temple was completely destroyed 40 years later. The fate of His people weighed heavily on Jesus that final week. By His miracle He proclaimed that doom was imminent. The merciful Jesus would gladly plead for a respite, but He knew it was now too late.

The Parable of the Barren Fig Tree

The miracle of the cursed fig tree occurs in Matthew and Mark but not in Luke. Luke's Gospel (13:6-9) carries a parable of warning against a barren fig tree not found in Matthew or Mark, so all three Gospels contain basically the same message. Jesus denounced spiritual barrenness by means of both parable and miracle. A miracle, you will recall, has been described as an acted parable.

● *Warning for everyone.* Though the primary application of the barren fig tree in both the miracle and the parable warns against a sterile Judaism in Jesus' day, the message extends to fruitless believers in every generation. Often Bible writers liken God's people to trees which are expected to bring forth fruit (Ps. 1:3; Matt. 7:15-20; John 15:1-7). Luke's parable says, "A certain man had a fig tree planted in his vineyard; and he came and sought fruit thereon, and found none. Then said he unto the dresser of his vineyard, 'Behold, these three years I come seeking fruit on this fig tree, and find none; cut it down; why cumbereth it the ground?' And he answering said unto him, 'Lord, let it alone this year also, till I shall dig about it, and dung it; and if it bear fruit, well; and if not, then after that thou shalt cut it down'" (13:6-9).

Believers Have Been Planted to Bear Fruit

When a farmer grows a fruit tree, he expects someday to find fruit on it. The divine Farmer wishes us to bear much fruit, which thereby brings glory to His name (John 15:8). Not to bear fruit brings disappointment and possible pruning.

The fruitful life shows itself in walking like Christ, working for Christ, and winning people to Christ. To rephrase it: The fruitful Christian has a gracious disposition, does godly deeds, and disciples others, helping them to believe on Christ and grow in Him.

● *Disposition.* After 30 years a faithful church usher was retiring. Instructing his successor in the details of the task, he concluded, "Remember we have nothing but gracious Christians in this congregation—till you try to put someone else in their pew!"

How easy to become unkind, gloomy, critical, bitter, envious, lukewarm, insensitive, rebellious, and impatient. Someone quipped, "There would be fewer pedestrian patients if there were more patient pedestrians."

A cartoon showed a wife speaking to her husband a few minutes before they left for the morning service. Apparently he had been acting rather cantankerously. She suggested, "Why don't you reverse your roles today? Be charming at home and grumpy at church." The fruit of the Spirit is "love, joy, peace, patience, kindness, goodness, faithfulness, gentleness, and self-control" (Gal. 5:22-23, NIV). Immediately after the miracle of the fig tree Jesus spoke of faith and forgiveness (Mark 11:22-23).

Fruitfulness involves Christlike living. A Spanish evangelist in Latin America, impeccably dressed in a white linen suit, was eating dinner in a restaurant before the evening service. Suddenly the waiter spilled soup on the evangelist's coat and trousers. Apologizing profusely, he cringed before the evangelist, for waiters had been known to lose their jobs through such carelessness. But the evangelist jumped to his feet and assured the waiter and the manager that all was well, even though it meant preaching in a soiled suit. When the evangelist returned to the same restaurant the next day, the waiter beckoned him to a side room, where he begged him to tell why he acted so kindly instead of letting loose with the usual torrent of oaths.

● *Deeds.* An inward Christlike disposition should express itself in outward Christlike deeds. Paul wanted the Colossians to live a life worthy of the Lord: "Bearing fruit in every good work" (1:10, NIV). The Apostle James gives an example of a good work: "Religion that God our Father accepts as pure and faultless is this: to look after orphans and widows" (1:27, NIV).

When two prize chickens wandered into a neighbor's vegetable garden, the neighbor wrung their necks and tossed them back over the owner's fence. The owner, seeing her chickens flung over the fence onto her lawn, ran out to the still-flopping birds. Her children wondered what their mother's reaction would be: angry denunciation of the ill-tempered neighbor, tears, or crying on Father's shoulder when he came home? To their amazement she proceeded to make two delicious chicken pies, one of which she took to the neighbor with an apology for the damage her chickens had done to his garden. The children, hiding behind a bush, saw their usually articulate neighbor standing speechless and ashamed.

● *Discipling.* When we are winsome, we may be used of God to win some. Seeing our Christlike behavior and actions, others may wish to know the source of our lifestyle. This opens the door to present the claims of Christ. Any listener who receives Christ would be spiritual fruit.

Three years after the sinking of the *Titanic,* a young Scotsman related in a church service in Hamilton, Canada that the night the ship went down he had been thrown into the icy waters. Somehow he had managed to grab a spar and hang on for dear life. He reported, "Suddenly a wave brought a man near me. He said his name was John Harper of Glasgow. He too was holding onto a piece of wreckage. He called out to me, 'Man, are you saved?' When I answered no, he shouted through the darkness, 'Believe on the Lord Jesus Christ, and thou shalt be saved.' The waves bore him away, then strangely a little later washed him alongside. 'Are you saved now?' he called out. When I replied I could not say yes, he repeated the same verse. Losing his grip on the spar, he sank. Alone in the night, with two miles of ocean under me, I trusted Christ as my Saviour. I am John Harper's last convert."

When an official of Moody Bible Institute heard this story later, he said, "I knew John Harper. He was on his way to this school when he drowned." Today a room in Chicago's Moody Church is called the Harper Room, named after this man whose courageous example and faithfulness unto death drew a fellow-traveler to Christ, who thus became John Harper's last spiritual fruit.

Believers Will Be Carefully Inspected

The parable tells how the owner of the fig tree came to look for fruit on it, but did not find any. He came not once but many times, inspecting it over a period of three years but in vain. Are you really bearing fruit for the Lord? Does He see any love, patience, and self-control? Not only at church, but in the office, school, and home? Is it evident to everyone that you are becoming fruitful to the praise of the Master Farmer?

● *The danger of fruitlessness.* The owner had a right to expect to find figs, but he was disappointed. For three years the tree had produced, not little figs, nor inferior figs, but no figs. John wrote, "I have no greater joy than to hear that my children walk in truth" (3 John 4). What a lovely sight to see God's people bowed down with the fruit of the Spirit, humbly serving the Lord. Since the owner could discover no fruit, he said, "Cut it down! Why should it use up the soil?" Why let a sterile tree sap nourishment from the ground, and rob others of sunshine and rain? Get rid of it to make room for another tree that will bear figs.

The purpose of the religious leaders was to shepherd and teach the people so that they would recognize the Messiah when He came. Because they were failing to do so, they were headed for destruction. When the Pharisees and Sadducees failed to bring forth the fruits that evidenced repentance, John the Baptist warned, "Now also the ax is laid unto the root of the tree; therefore every tree which bringest not forth good fruit is hewn down, and cast into the fire" (Matt. 3:10). Speaking of fruitless branches, Jesus said, "Men gather them, and cast them into the fire, and they are burned" (John 15:6).

Uselessness invites disaster. The Master expects a harvest of fruit. When a professing believer fails to fulfill his or her function, that person has become redundant, and is in danger of doom. Therein lies the tragedy of barrenness. The Master has a right to destroy what does not produce fruit.

● *The hypocrisy of fruitlessness.* The doomed fig tree had appearance without performance. The luxuriant foliage had caught the Saviour's eye, but it was attractiveness without reality. The leaves were nothing but a front to hide the emptiness beneath. It was profession without possession. The Lord should have been received by His people, but they rejected Him. Jesus scathed the Pharisees for their hypocrisy, accusing them of not only swindling widows out of their property, but of covering up their cheating with long prayers; He added, "Such men will be punished most severely" (Mark 12:40). He accused them of tithing the smallest of plants while neglecting major virtues like justice, mercy, and faithfulness. He likened them to whitewashed tombs, which look beautiful on the outside but on the inside are full of dead men's bones and everything unclean. "In the same way," He said, "on the outside you appear to people as righteous but on the inside are full of hypocrisy and wickedness" (Matt. 23:23, 27). Their harvest of righteousness turned out to be a hoax.

How quickly we identify in secular life the inconsistency of people who fail to practice what they preach: peddlers selling signs door-to-door which read, "No Peddlers Allowed"; the author of a best-selling book on how to make a fortune by investing in real estate filing for bankruptcy; a tax expert who taught a course on federal taxation sentenced for tax evasion.

Much more tragic loom the incongruities of professing Christians whose behavior does not match their beliefs: a college student sharing his faith with a fellow-student, then later cheating on an exam; a husband too busy preparing a Sunday School lesson on helpfulness to lend his wife a helping hand in a small task; a deacon who quotes chapter and verse to all around but who makes it miserable for his wife. Outsiders readily recognize the leaves of pious profession. They say, "Those church members are no different from the people who make no profession at all. They have no love, no unselfishness, no long-suffering. Their tempers are just as ugly and violent as anybody else's. They're as difficult to live with, and pull just as sharp and shrewd dealings as anyone else."

Also God, before whom our inner secrets are naked and open, and before whom we all must give account, will see beneath all leaves of hypocrisy covering up the barrenness of our hearts.

Believers Must Exercise Constant Self-Discipline

This miracle, besides warning against a barren and hypocritical life, also points out the patience of the God of another chance. When the owner of the fig tree found no fruit for three years, the dresser of the vineyard pled for "one more year, and I'll dig around it and fertilize it. If it bears fruit next year, fine! If not, then cut it down" (Luke 13:8-9, NIV).

God is so patient, as He was in the days of Noah, the judges, the kings, the first century, and today. Though the Lord Jesus intercedes for us at God's right hand, He expects us to take advantage of all means of grace to cultivate our spiritual life. Peter commands us to diligently add to our faith virtue, knowledge, self-control, patience, godliness, brotherly kindness, and love. The possession of these qualities proves fruitfulness. But their absence indicates forgetfulness of our cleansing from past sins (2 Peter 1:5-9). Paul said, "I keep under my body, and bring it into subjection; lest that by any means when I have preached to others, I myself should be a castaway" (1 Cor. 9:27). He did not fear loss of his salvation, but he was concerned lest he not bear fruit and become an instrument unsuited for the Lord's service. If no fruit, judgment in the form of removal from service would fall.

If you have felt the Master's sharp knife in your life, He may want you to think more deeply about the things of God. Maybe He is dealing with you in that extra year of grace. How prone we are to wander and leave the God we love. In an apocryphal parable attributed to Jesus, the kingdom of God is likened to a woman carrying a jar of porridge. As she walks on the road to her house, the jar develops a leak. The porridge dribbles out behind her on the road. Not till arriving home does she find her jar empty. How easy through little disobedience, little lapses of morality, little carelessnesses in devotional practices, little absences from public worship, and little coldnesses in our service to suddenly find that we have no fruit but only leaves remaining. Each day we need to abide in Christ, trusting Him to produce the fruit of His likeness in us.

12

BACK FROM
THE DEAD

I n her book *Can Somebody Shout Amen?* (Thomas Dunne, 1988) Patsy Sims devotes 25 pages to an attempted raising from the dead in Tennessee in 1981. Tommy Walker, Jr. drowned on a June Saturday. The local rescue squad soon recovered the body and took it to a nearby hospital where the 19-year-old lad was pronounced dead. His father, a minister, and the boy's mother refused to accept their son's death. Convinced that God would raise their boy from the dead, they wanted to take his body home. After the authorities refused to release the corpse to anyone but an undertaker, the Walkers persuaded a local mortician to let them take it.

At home, the couple and Timothy, their 17-year-old son, began praying and fasting. As news of the vigil spread, hundreds of people came to the house, some to pray, others to observe. The next two evening services conducted by Timothy in a tent attracted overflow audiences. The vigil continued into the third day. At 4 o'clock that Monday morning, Mrs. Walker realized that the corpse had started to decompose, and awoke her husband. They scheduled a viewing at the undertaker's that evening, and the funeral for 11:30 next morning.

The service started an hour earlier than announced. Beat-up cars and trucks with bumper stickers declaring "God is my pilot" lined the highway. Across from the tent a sign announced, "Funeral for Tommy Walker, Jr.—Tues. 9:00–11:30 A.M.—Here." Uniformed policemen moved about the tent and up and down the roadside. The platform was jammed with musicians. The hearse was backed up close to the tent, waiting for the pallbearers to place the casket therein, but the people were not yet ready to surrender their belief that God would raise Tommy, Jr. For more than three hours they petitioned God with no sign of stopping. More people surrounded the tent. The casket, closed and without flowers, stood in front of the platform.

This was now the fourth day. A strange mixture of expectancy and hopelessness filled the air. Yet the usual signs of sorrow were absent. Mrs. Walker was at the organ and her husband at the pulpit, just as in a typical service. Those unaware of the situation would never have thought their son lay in that coffin. Buoyant and smiling, neither evidenced any manifestations of grief. Pastor Walker said that God could still, at that very moment, raise Tommy from the cold, metallic-blue coffin. The father invited all who believed God could raise Tommy to come and lay hands on the casket. The people pressed forward toward the casket, a mass of arms, legs, and bodies.

Walker prayed, "I thank You, Lord, that You're a dead-raiser. I thank You for raising my son from the dead!" Everyone seemed oblivious both to the harsh reality of the motionless body in the casket and to the incongruity of his prayer. After eulogizing his son and warning his hearers of the uncertainty of life, he stated God had given him a revelation that morning that Tommy was singing around the throne in heaven and would not now be raised from the dead. He added, "Everybody that's going to the cemetery just get in line. Amen."

Six teenagers lined up on either side of the coffin and carried it to the waiting hearse. Cars slowly followed the sleek limousine down a steep, winding road that led to the cemetery. The casket was laid under a green canopy, next to a pile of freshly turned earth. After more remarks the undertaker signaled the pallbearers, who then lowered the casket into the ground. The parents walked away from the graveside convinced that, though it was not to be in the case of their son, God does indeed raise the dead.

Does God raise the dead today? We know He can, but does He? It does not seem to be normative. Investigation of some reported resurrections indicate that the people did not really die. Even though vital signs were absent, they were cases of resuscitation. In other instances, we hear of someone supposedly dying in a hospital, being declared dead prematurely, then awakening in a mortuary. About 20 years ago stories of dramatic raisings in Indonesia circulated in Christian circles. Dr. Stanley Mooneyham, then president of World Vision, wrote, "Were people raised from the dead? There is not one medically confirmed case. The two or three cases to which they would give some credence involved persons having been 'dead' only a few hours. If trained doctors are unable to agree on when a person is clinically dead, how should these people be expected to make that critical judgment?" ("Revival and Miracles—What about Indonesia?" *World Vision,* September 1972) Most supposed raisings occur soon after death. The raising of a person dead several days, like Lazarus, would be much more convincing, and certainly within the power of God, if in His sovereignty He chose to do so.

Turning from disputed cases of dead-raising, we do know from the Gospels of three people Jesus raised during His ministry: the son of the widow of Nain, Jairus' daughter, and Jesus' friend Lazarus.

The Son of the Widow of Nain

Luke gives the only record of Jesus coming upon a funeral procession (7:11-15). Leaving Capernaum, Jesus traveled 25 miles to Nain, a village 6 miles southwest of Nazareth, accompanied by His disciples and a great crowd.

As Jesus and His followers approached the village gate, they met a funeral cortege emerging from Nain to bury a young man at a cemetery a short walk outside the village. The body was carried on a flat board or in a wicker basket. Face uncovered and hands folded made the dead person appear as if asleep. In the crowd of mourners were the friends, the professional wailing women, a host of men and boys, and most poignantly of all, the mother of the dead youth.

When Jesus saw the mourning mother, He was moved with compassion. How vividly she recalled her son's baby days and his growing period when she kissed away his hurts and watched over him with high hopes. He was her only son. And she was a widow with no husband to comfort her. Jesus had a soft spot in His heart for widows, perhaps because His mother was one. Also, with her only support gone, she would be economically deprived. Despite the crowd about her, she was all alone. Today amid crowded funeral viewings, slowly wending funeral processions, and graveside farewells, many a heart weeps all alone.

Jesus is no mere or remote spectator simply observing human affairs. He is touched with the feelings of our infirmities. Jesus cares! He said to the heartbroken widow, "Do not weep." Then He touched the bier to halt the procession and indicated to the pallbearers to set it down. With one simple gesture He brought the frenzied mob to a quiet stop. Without touching the body or taking the dead youth's hand, Jesus spoke, "Young man, I say unto you, arise." The youth sat up and began to speak. Effortlessly, he was fully restored to life. The miracle restored not only life but health. He had completely recovered. At that point Jesus presented her son alive, well, and probably erect. Awestruck, the people hailed Him as a great prophet.

The Raising of Jairus' Daughter

The restoration of life to the daughter of Jairus is the only miracle of Jesus' raising the dead recorded in more than one Gospel; it appears in the three Synoptics (Matt. 9:18-19, 23-26; Mark 5:21-24, 35-43; Luke 8:40-42, 49-56).

155

Synagogues usually had a board of seven members. Jairus, one of the rulers of the Capernaum synagogue, who knew Jesus because of His participation in the local services, had a great need. Waiting for Jesus to return to Capernaum following His healing of the Gadarene demoniac on the other side of the lake, Jairus approached the Saviour in desperation. With the synagogues rapidly closing their doors on Jesus, how significant that Jairus stifled his pride and came begging. Just as significant was Jesus' lack of resentment for the rulers' rejection. He could have responded, "You've banished Me from your synagogues. Why come to me in your trouble?" But Jesus bore no grudges.

Jairus' 12-year-old daughter was dying. Before Jesus could get to the ruler's house, she would die. The only child in the family—how her parents would miss her!

He pled, "My little daughter is at the point of death. Come and lay Your hands on her, so that she may be made well, and live." Now began the seesaw of faith. His faith was reassured when Jesus started walking with him toward his home. But his faith was tested by a delay. A woman with an issue of blood touched the hem of Jesus' garment, looking for a cure. Jesus stopped to bring her into open confession. Would Jesus ever start out again? When the woman was gloriously healed, Jairus' faith took an upward swing. But then came the tragic news, "Your daughter is dead. Why trouble the Teacher any further?" His faith dipped. Then Jesus said, "Don't be afraid. Just believe, and she will be healed." His faith soared.

When Jesus arrived at Jairus' house, He found great turmoil. The weeping of relatives and the wailing of professional mourners mingled with the plaintive sound of flutes. Rebuking the mourners, He asked, "Why do you make a tumult and weep? The child is not dead but sleeping." They laughed in scorn. Jesus hadn't even seen the girl and was presuming to imagine at a distance something those close to her knew for sure. Jesus was referring to her body, which looked asleep, not to her spirit. Jesus was not denying the reality of her death, nor teaching that death should be considered sleep. Rather He was using figurative language to indicate that for this girl death was like sleep because it was not permanent but would end in an awakening.

Jesus ordered the mourners out, letting only her parents, Peter, James, and John enter the room where the body lay. He wanted witnesses to know what He was about to do. Taking the lifeless child by the hand, He said, "Little girl, I say to you, get up!" Immediately, her spirit returned. The little girl rose up and walked. Jesus told them to give her something to eat, then ordered the astonished parents and three disciples not to tell anyone what had happened. But who could keep such an astounding miracle to himself? The news spread like wildfire through the whole area.

The Raising of Lazarus

Jesus and the Twelve, temporarily beyond Jordan because of serious threats back in Judea, received word of an emergency in Bethany (see John 11:1-44). Sisters Martha and Mary sent a message that their brother Lazarus, whom Jesus loved, was seriously sick. They thought Jesus would come immediately and exercise His healing power on their brother, but He waited two more days in the same place. Jesus continued His tasks far from the worried sisters who alternated between caring for Lazarus and looking down the road to see if the Master was coming. To their utter bewilderment Jesus did not come. Lazarus became worse and died. In the meantime Jesus told His disciples plainly that Lazarus was dead, and that they should then go to him. Pessimistically, Thomas said, "Let's go that we may die with Jesus." Were they not plunging back into the middle of trouble, going so close to Jerusalem? And just to visit a corpse!

By the time they reached Bethany, Lazarus had been four days in the grave, his body beginning to decompose. The ritual of mourning had already peaked. Martha, hearing Jesus was in the vicinity, hurried out to meet Him. Her first words reflected a classic response to a hopeless situation: "How different things would have turned out, Jesus, if You had come in time." Then Jesus spoke a word of encouragement, "Your brother will rise again." Martha responded by putting the solution in the future, "I know he will rise in the resurrection at the last day." But Jesus spoke to her of a present hope, "I am the resurrection and the life." Martha replied with a great confession, "I believe that You are the Christ, the Son of God, who was to come into the world."

Martha then left Jesus to tell Mary that the Master had arrived. Mary greeted Jesus with the same comment, "If You had been here, my brother would not have died." The group of comforters at the house followed. Deeply moved in spirit, Jesus asked, "Where have you laid him?" They replied, "Come and see." Then Jesus wept. Down those holy cheeks trickled tears in genuine sorrow over the loss of His friend and in genuine sympathy with Martha and Mary in their bereavement.

At the tomb Jesus said, "Take away the stone." Martha said, "By this time there's a strong odor, for he's been there four days." Jesus replied, "Did I not tell you that if you believed, you would see the glory of God?" They removed the stone. Jesus prayed, thanking His Heavenly Father for always hearing Him. Then He cried with a loud voice, "Lazarus, come forth!" A country preacher commented, "If Jesus hadn't limited that command to Lazarus, every corpse in the graveyard would have come forth. It was just Lazarus this time. Someday it will be everybody."

Suddenly Lazarus stood erect and staggered out of the tomb, all wrapped up like a mummy. At Jesus' word they unwound him. What a party as they hugged him and danced around for joy.

These three raisings gave a little preview of larger events to come. First, they anticipated the raisings on the first Easter morning when the bodies of many saints which slept arose, came out of their graves, went into the city of Jerusalem, and appeared to many (Matt. 27:52-53). Second, they foreshadowed the final resurrection when all in graves shall come forth. Third, these three raisings have a symbolic meaning.

Just as the healing of the blind symbolizes Jesus' capability to open our eyes to the Light of the world, and just as the healing of the deaf portrays Jesus' power to give divine understanding to the mind, and just as the healing of the lame shows how Jesus can restore our disabled faculties so we can walk in righteousness, so the three raisings picture His ability to give spiritual life to those who are dead in trespasses and sins.

All Three Needed Life

An Alfred Hitchcock TV episode depicted a wicked woman sentenced to life imprisonment for murder. She concocted a plan to escape. After making friends with an old inmate who assisted in the burial of prisoners who died, she bribed him to help her get out. Next time she heard the toll of the bell which signaled the death of an inmate, she was to slip down to the workroom where he made the caskets, locate the casket in which he had placed the corpse, quietly slide herself into the same casket, and pull the lid down tightly. Early the next morning the old man would roll her, along with the corpse inside, on an old cart, through the gate to the cemetery just outside. Next day he would return, and let her out.

Late one night she heard the bell toll. She slid off her cot, crept to the dimly lit room, spotted the coffin, squeezed in beside the corpse, and pulled the lid down tightly. A few hours later she could sense the wheels rolling, feel the box lowering, and hear the dirt hitting the top of the casket. Though sealed beneath the ground, she would soon be released. Her elation slowly faded as the hours went by. Where was the old man? In panic she lit a match. She was terrified to discover that next to her was the old man himself who had died. Doomed, she would soon die. In the meantime she would be the living among the dead.

It's possible for the same person to be alive, yet dead: alive physically, but dead from the standpoint of enthusiasm. This notice appeared in a company memorandum posted on an office bulletin board. "It has come to the attention of the management that workers dying on the job are failing to fall down. This practice must stop, as it becomes impossible to distinguish between death and the natural movement of the staff. Any employee found dead in the upright position will be dropped from the payroll." This notice reminds one of the

epitaph on a gravestone, "He died at 48, was buried at 72."
An epitaph on a pastor's monument read:

"Go tell the Church that I'm dead
But they need shed no tears;
For though I'm dead I'm no more dead
Than they have been for years."

In our natural condition we are dead in trespasses and sins
(Eph. 2:1, 5). What we need is the power of the Gospel to
give us newness of life: spiritual life. Interestingly, Paul declares that what it takes to give us spiritual life is the same
power required to raise Jesus from the dead. Paul prayed that
we might know "His incomparably great power" which is "like
the working of His mighty strength, which He exerted in
Christ when He raised Him from the dead" (Eph. 1:19-20,
NIV).

Through disobedience to God, our first parents lost their
right to the tree of life. Spiritual death occurred at the moment
of rebellion. Everyone born since then possesses a nature
that's not alive to God and His matters. An open-air preacher
was interrupted by a youth who yelled out, "You talk about a
burden of sin. I feel none." Then he flippantly added, "How
much does sin weigh? Eighty pounds? Ten pounds?" The
preacher retorted, "Tell me, if you laid a 400-pound weight on
a dead man's chest, would he feel it?" Replied the youth, "No,
because he's dead." The preacher countered, "And the man
who feels no load of sin is dead spiritually."

A preacher, riding in the front seat of a hearse, wanted to
witness to the funeral director who was leading a procession of
cars to the cemetery. He quoted Jesus' words, "Let the dead
bury their dead" (Matt. 8:22), then explained to the puzzled
mortician that people who have physical life may not possess
spiritual life. If those without spiritual life take part in burial
services, then the spiritually dead are burying the physically
dead.

An outsider was buried in a church graveyard. Greatly agitated by this event, the members put up a notice which read,

"This graveyard is reserved for the dead who are living in this parish." Many living folk are really dead. Paul wrote, "She that liveth in pleasure is dead while she liveth" (1 Tim. 5:6).

Just as the widow of Nain's son, Jairus' daughter, and Lazarus all needed physical life, so every member of the human race needs spiritual life. That's why Jesus visited earth. He said, "I am come that they might have life" (John 10:10). His conversation with Nicodemus revealed that the way to spiritual life is through the new birth. Those who believe on Him now have eternal life, have passed from death to life (5:24), and have their names in the Book of Life (Rev. 20:12).

People of All Ages Needed Spiritual Life

Jairus' daughter was a child. The widow's son was a youth, perhaps in his late teens or early twenties. Lazarus was a mature man, in the prime of life.

● *Childhood.* At 12 years of age, the little girl had reached an important age in Jewish life. Tradition says that at 12, Samuel heard the call of God in the temple; that at 12, Solomon made his request for wisdom; and Scripture tells us that at 12, Jesus confounded the doctors in the temple.

Preadolescent children have made lasting decisions for Christ, among them hymn writers P.P. Bliss and Isaac Watts and missionaries David Brainerd and Robert Moffat. Jonathan Edwards came to Christ at the age of seven, and Corrie ten Boom and Evangelist Leighton Ford both at five. Norman B. Rohrer in his book *Leighton Ford: A Life Surprised* tells of Leighton sitting on the front seat at a children's "Happy Hour" at Canadian Keswick and raising his hand in response to the invitation to salvation. The teacher whispered, "You're too young." After a second invitation Leighton's small hand shot up. Again she tried to dissuade him. When he raised his hand the third time, the teacher perceived that the lad of five genuinely comprehended what he was doing (Tyndale House, 1981, p. 26).

● *Youth.* Just as the youthful son of the widow of Nain

needed physical life, so all young people need spiritual life. The style of life bombarding youth from TV with its violence, drugs, alcohol, and illicit sex, plus peer pressure, makes it difficult for young people to live godly lives. Also, adolescence is a time for important decisions, such as "What career will I follow?" "What college will I attend?" "Whom will I marry?" How wonderful for early teenagers to have Christ as both Saviour and Lord to guide them through those tempestuous adolescent years. When the prodigal son returned from his waywardness, his father said of him that he "was dead and is alive again" (Luke 15:32, RSV).

● *Mature people.* Perhaps Lazarus was in his 30s. He represents all the people in the prime of life and older who need eternal life. Literally millions never attend church services except at Christmas or Easter. When asked how near to a church he lived and how long it took him to get there, a man responded with an answer that could be typical, "I live four blocks away, and it takes me six months to get there." On any Sunday morning millions are lounging at home after sleeping late, or plodding through the Sunday paper, or going out to eat, or to the beach or a football game. With no interest in eternal matters, they are spiritually dead.

All Received Spiritual Life through Jesus

None of these people was raised by means of a pulmotor or mouth-to-mouth resuscitation. Rather, all were raised through the voice of Jesus. "Little girl, I say to you, get up!" "Young man, I say to you, get up." "Lazareth, come out!" Also, in the final resurrection day the dead shall hear His voice and come forth.

Similarly, it's the word of the Lord that gives spiritual life. Jesus said that "whoever hears My word and believes" has eternal life (John 5:24). He also stated that "the words I have spoken to you are spirit and they are life" (6:63). James wrote, "He chose to give us birth through the word of truth" (1:18, NIV).

Interestingly, the raisings seemed to involve different degrees of difficulty. The little girl was still on her deathbed. The young man, in his funeral procession, was on his way to burial. Lazarus had been in the grave four days. The little girl had been dead about a half hour, the man about half a day, and Lazarus about half a week. It might have seemed easier to raise the little girl or youth, so recently dead, than Lazarus, who had been dead for four days. Yet it took as much power to raise each one, for each was as lifeless as the other. It takes just as much divine power to regenerate a respectable, self-righteous, religious person as it does a derelict or criminal.

● *Great change.* For all three, breath, pulse, and color returned. In Lazarus' case, he changed his clothes, a word often translated "habits." His company and environment were different. No longer did he waste away in the grave with the dead as his companions. When we receive spiritual life, our habits should change. We should seek the company of other alive-in-Christ brothers and sisters that comprise the family of God. When Augustine was converted by the Word of Christ, his new life displayed itself in a new relationship with his mother. New babes in Christ should begin to restore broken relationships, replacing animosity with fellowship. Lazarus' restoration proved a great attraction, drawing a crowd not only to see Jesus but Lazarus as well, living proof of Jesus' power. Our behavior should pulsate with Christlike living, winsomely drawing people to the Saviour. On the other hand, the presence of Lazarus raised the opposition of Jesus' enemies who then wanted to get rid of both Jesus and Lazarus. The uprightness of our new lives also often draws the hostility of the unrighteous.

● *Help needed.* In the custom of the day Lazarus had been wrapped in long swathes of linen. Since legs were wrapped separately, these graveclothes did not prevent him from walking, but they hampered full freedom of movement. That's why Jesus said, "Loose him and let him go." Removing the napkin around his head would permit his speech to be unmuffled and his eyes to see.

When new converts come forth from their spiritual graves,

163

they are usually encumbered with the graveclothes of their old lives. They need the support of mature Christians to get rid of the old habits and grow in the freedom of the Gospel. Regeneration needs to be followed by sanctification, a lifelong process of putting off the old nature and putting on the new man.

In Washington, D.C. stands the National Episcopal Cathedral with its many beautiful stained-glass windows, one of which portrays the tender face of the Good Shepherd. The artist who painted that kind face told me that for his model he used a man who had been an alcoholic derelict from Philadelphia. Many a night the man had slept in alleys with a brick for a pillow. On winter mornings he had often had to pull his frozen beard away from the brick. One day he staggered through the swinging doors of what he thought was a saloon but which turned out to be a rescue mission. He heard the Gospel, received Christ, was reunited with his family, and later became superintendent of that same mission. When the stained-glass artist was looking for a model from which to paint the Good Shepherd's face, he chose this man. This former derelict, once dead in trespasses and sins, was given newness of life in Christ. He was indeed—*back from the dead.*

AFTERWORD

T he supreme miracle worker of all centuries, the Lord Jesus Christ, decisively and repeatedly demonstrated His power over nature, disease, and death.

What do these miracles of Jesus mean to you?

His miracles should signify to you that He was indeed the very Son of God, the appointed messenger from on High, who spoke with the Father's authority, and whose word was to be obeyed.

Not only should His wonders signal the deity of the Lord Jesus, but they should also lead you to receive eternal life through faith in Him (John 20:30-31).

The miracles should also impress you with the Master's mercy. Never for His own advancement did Jesus perform a miracle. He never jumped off the temple pinnacle to show off, nor did He ever turn stones into bread to satisfy His own hunger. He never did a miracle capriciously, trivially, or malevolently. Rather, we are told that compassion moved Him to heal the sick, feed the hungry, and raise the dead. The miracles should lead you to a deeper appreciation of His loving kindness.

Then, the miracles should picture for you how God's saving grace can cure the spiritual ills that beset the human race. Of course, these were real physical maladies that oppressed people, and they were genuine healings. But the physical illnesses were symbolic of the spiritual ills that hold the human race in its grip, and the healings were emblematic of the spiritual transformations available to you today. Though the miracles possess these apologetic, evangelistic, and merciful purposes, the symbolic significance has been the main thrust of this book. Repeatedly we have stated that the cleansing of the leper illustrates the removal of defilement from spiritual outcasts. The healing of sightless eyes portrays the giving of spiritual sight to those blinded by sin. And the raising of the dead pictures the giving of spiritual life to those dead in sin. The miracles should encourage you to expect spiritual victories in areas of present defeat in your life.

An Assembly of God Revivaltime Radio sermon of 1987 told of Rich, a new believer, on his way out of church after a sermon on the futility of bitterness and revenge, who told the pastor, "I didn't agree with that message. There's a man I hate. I'll never forgive him for what he did to me."

The pastor learned that a year before, Rich had been closing his store around 9 P.M. when a tall gunman, a silk stocking over his face, placed the barrel of a .38 pistol between Rich's eyes, and pulled the trigger. The gun clicked but didn't fire. Puzzled, he aimed the gun at the front window and pulled the trigger again. With a deafening roar the plate glass shattered into the street. Angry, the gunman brought the gun butt down so hard on Rich's skull that pieces of his skull penetrated the membrane surrounding the brain. The gunman pushed Judy, Rich's wife, away from the cash register, and taking the cash, disappeared into the dark.

Rushed to a hospital near Cleveland, Rich underwent surgery and his life was spared, though recovery was slow. The gunman was later captured and sentenced to 25 years in an Ohio prison. Soon after, Rich and Judy became believers. Now, during a sermon on forgiveness Rich could think only of the man who had tried to kill him. He would never forgive that man!

But the couple kept growing in grace. One day Rich nervously showed his pastor a letter bearing a prison address. It began, "Dear Rich, I am the man who tried to kill you." It said that he deserved to be in prison, but that he had given his life to Christ, and was now asking Rich to forgive him for the terrible thing he had done. It ended, "I ask for nothing else— just your forgiveness. Thank you. Your friend, Artie."

Rich asked the pastor what he should do. When the pastor replied, "You're supposed to forgive him," Rich picked up the letter and stormed out repeating, "Never—he tried to kill me!"

A few months later Rich asked the pastor to pray for him and Judy, for on the following Thursday, they were driving down to the prison to see Artie. When Rich and Artie met, they virtually ran into each other's arms, then stood there weeping as the other prisoners stared in astonishment.

Rich commented to the pastor, "Artie is a pretty fine fellow once you get to know him," this coming from the man who so recently had expressed such intense hatred for his attacker. Thereafter, the couple spent many Thursdays driving to the prison to visit Artie.

One day Rich broke the news that they were trying to get Artie released. The amazed pastor said it would be impossible since the prisoner had served only 2 years, when at least 16 years had to be served before any consideration of parole.

A few months later, Rich phoned the pastor. "Judy and I want to have lunch with you and your wife at the restaurant next Thursday at noon. Make reservations for five." The pastor asked who the fifth person was. After a pause came the reply, "Artie! He's being released into our custody Thursday morning."

The dumbfounded pastor asked, "Where will he ever find work? And where will he live? The law says he must have a permanent address." Rich replied, "I have made Artie a partner in my business. He'll be living with us in our home!"

The pastor protested, "Think it through. A criminal, convicted of attempted murder, and you have three precious little girls in your home." But Rich wouldn't let him say any more. "Pastor, that was another man. Artie is a new creature."

Fourteen years later, when Revivaltime broadcast this story, Artie was no longer working for Rich or living in his home. He was living with his own wife and children in Cleveland, Ohio and was a minister of the Gospel. Incidentally, one of the men is white; the other is black.

What God did for Rich and Artie, He is able to do for you.

THE MIRACLES OF JESUS

Artie, defiled with the leprosy of dishonesty and violence, was cleansed by the power of Christ, and enabled to live a life of rectitude and gentleness. Rich, crippled with revenge and bitterness, was made to walk the path of forgiveness. Both men, blind to areas of need in their lives, came to see. And both, dead in sin, came alive in righteousness. For you, it's a matter of your asking the supreme miracle worker to forgive your sin on the basis of His sacrifice on the cross.

But there's still another significance of Jesus' miracles for you. They have a prophetic purpose—to declare the ultimate triumph of God's kingdom over the forces of evil, including disease, demonic influence, and death. If you are a male 50 years of age, healthy, living in the USA, you can anticipate living into your early 70s, based on average life expectancy; average American females can expect to live 7 years longer than that. But if you were an Ethiopian, you would have died, on average, 13 years ago. If a Cambodian, 9 years ago. If a Mozambican, 7 years ago. If a Haitian, 6 years ago. A Bengali or Zairian, last year.

But because of Christ's death 19 centuries ago, all who put their trust in Him will someday have perfect bodies which will never die. True—during our earthly pilgrimage the Lord may sometimes intervene to heal in a miraculous manner, but sooner or later all of us will die. So, the miracles provide a foretaste of a coming age when Jesus Christ will completely subdue the forces of Satan in a cosmic mop-up, and usher in a new heaven and a new earth. What a prospect—no panting of cardiacs, no gasping of emphysema sufferers, no crippling of arthritics, no wasting of cancer victims, no pain, no sickness, no darkness, no hunger, no thirst, no demons, no death!

Are you in need of a spiritual transformation? The supreme miracle worker is still opening the ears of those deaf to His word, stilling the storm in human hearts, and giving eternal life to those devoid of spiritual vitality.

And if you have loved ones who have spiritual needs, recall how Jesus, seeing the faith of those who brought the paralyzed man to Him, told the paralytic to take up his bed and walk. Don't give up. Keep bringing your friends to Jesus.